Praise for *Prepare Th...*

The church possesses a unique responsibility to identify leaders among God's people and equip them for ministry among all peoples. As the Holy Spirit sets men apart for ministry, the local community of faith is accountable to God for training them up and sending them out in a way that glorifies Christ. I am thankful to Brian Croft for this immensely helpful, thoroughly biblical, and extremely practical resource that will serve well those called by God, their pastors, and their churches.

David Platt, senior pastor of The Church at Brook Hills, Birmingham, Alabama, and author of Radical

We live in an individualistic world where subjective and private experiences are often thought to be beyond contradiction. If someone claims he is called to ministry, who are we to doubt it? Brian Croft demonstrates, however, that an internal call to ministry must be matched by an external call. The people of God, the church of Jesus Christ, should play a major role in assessing whether someone is called to ministry. *Prepare Them to Shepherd* is biblically grounded and full of wise pastoral advice. I commend it enthusiastically.

Thomas R. Schreiner, James Buchanan Harrison professor of New Testament interpretation at The Southern Baptist Theological Seminary

Brian Croft loves the Savior, and he loves the church. That comes through on every page of this book. For those who care that the harvest is plentiful and want the Lord of the harvest to send workers, this book helps us to be sure the workers are worth their wages. Croft tells us what to look for — and when we find it, how to cultivate it.

Thabiti Anyabwile, senior pastor of First Baptist Church, Grand Cayman, and author of What Is a Healthy Church Member?

Pastor Croft has led his church to develop an intentional approach to evaluating a man's sense of call. If you have responsibilities of spiritual leadership in your local church, you'll want to get this book, for you'll find it helpful every time a man indicates that he senses God's call to vocational ministry.

Donald Whitney, associate professor of biblical spirituality at The Southern Baptist Theological Seminary

What Brian Croft has written will help pastors, churches, seminary professors, and students include an important but often-missed step in a man's journey from a mysterious call to the ministry to a local congregation's call of that man to a pastorate. Vocational and lay leaders should keep this work close at hand when a man professes an inward call to ministry.

Eric C. Redmond, executive pastoral assistant and Bible professor in residence at New Canaan Baptist Church, Washington, DC

When Paul wrote to the Galatians, he expected those churches to be able to discern whether the true gospel was being preached or whether what they were hearing was another gospel—even if the preacher was Paul himself or an angel from heaven! Brian Croft calls churches to take up responsibilities Paul expected them to exercise and pastors to do the kind of work Paul charged Timothy and Titus to do.

Jim Hamilton, associate professor of biblical theology at The Southern Baptist Theological Seminary and senior pastor of Kenwood Baptist Church

In *Prepare Them to Shepherd*, Brian Croft provides much-needed biblical discernment for ordinary pastors like myself. Pastor, read it to benefit your soul. Read it to equip your church. Read it to be amazed that you serve the Chief Shepherd.

Brian Chesemore, pastor of Sovereign Grace Church, Louisville, Kentucky

Brian Croft has helpfully heralded a call to local churches to return to the ownership of pastoral discipleship. *Prepare Them to Shepherd* will offer great clarity where much confusion has been found in recent years.

Eric Bancroft, senior pastor of Castleview Baptist Church, Indianapolis, Indiana

Brian Croft highlights the church's responsibility to call and affirm individuals who claim a personal, divine draw to the ministry. This undermines the highly individualistic sense of call that people speak about today, which is considered above evaluation or critique. This book will change minds about how we, as the body of Christ, affirm the pastoral ministry of individuals.

D. Jeffrey Mooney, senior pastor of First Baptist Church, Norco, California, and assistant professor of Christian studies at California Baptist University

PREPARE THEM TO SHEPHERD

REVISED AND UPDATED

Test, Train, Affirm, and Send the Next Generation of Pastors

Previously published as *Test, Train, Affirm, and Send into Ministry*

BRIAN CROFT

ZONDERVAN

Prepare Them to Shepherd
Copyright © 2014 by Brian Croft

Previously published in 2010 by Day One Publications under the title
Test, Train, Affirm, and Send into Ministry

This title is also available as a Zondervan ebook.
Visit www.zondervan.com/ebooks.

Requests for information should be addressed to:

Zondervan, 3900 *Sparks Dr. SE, Grand Rapids, Michigan* 49546

Library of Congress Cataloging-in-Publication Data

Croft, Brian.
        Prepare them to shepherd : test, train, affirm, and send the next
    generation of pastors / Brian Croft.
            p. cm. — (Practical shepherding series)
        ISBN 978-0-310-51716-0 (softcover)
        1. Clergy — Post-ordination training. 2. Discipling (Christianity)
    3. Theology — Study and teaching (Continuing education). I. Title.
    BV4165.C76 2014
    253 — dc23   2013041294

Cover design and illustrations: Jay Smith-Juicebox Designs
Interior design: Matthew Van Zomeren

Printed in the United States of America

HB 02.19.2024

To my brother, Scott,
who first challenged me
to seek and value the external call

CONTENTS

FOREWORD

HAS GOD CALLED YOU TO MINISTRY? Though all Christians are called to serve the cause of Christ, God calls certain persons to serve the church as pastors and other ministers. Writing to young Timothy, the apostle Paul confirmed that if a man aspires to be a pastor, "it is a fine work he desires to do" (1 Timothy 3:1 NASB). Likewise, it is a high honor to be called by God into the ministry of the church. How do you know if God is calling you?

First, there is an *inward* call. Through his Spirit, God speaks to those persons he has called to serve as pastors and ministers of his church. The great Reformer Martin Luther described this inward call as "God's voice heard by faith." Those whom God has called know this call by a sense of leading, purpose, and growing commitment.

Charles Spurgeon identified the first sign of God's call to the ministry as "an intense, all-absorbing desire for the work." Those called by God sense a growing compulsion to preach and teach the word, and to minister to the people of God.

This sense of compulsion should prompt the believer to consider whether God may be calling him to the ministry. Has God gifted you with the fervent desire to preach? Has he equipped you with the gifts necessary for ministry? Do you love God's word and feel called to teach? Spurgeon warned those who sought his counsel not to preach if they could help it. "But," Spurgeon continued, "if he cannot help it, and he must preach or die, then he is the man." That sense of urgent commission is one of the central marks of an authentic call.

Second, there is the *external* call. Baptists believe that God uses the congregation to "call out the called" to ministry. The congregation must evaluate and affirm the calling and gifts of the believer who feels called to the ministry. As a family of faith, the congregation should recognize and celebrate the gifts of ministry given to its members and take responsibility to encourage those whom God has called to respond to that call with joy and submission.

These days, many persons think of careers rather than callings. The biblical challenge to "consider your call" should be extended from the call to salvation to the call to the ministry. John Newton, famous for writing "Amazing Grace," once remarked that "none but he who made the world can make a minister of the gospel." Only God can call a true minister, and only he can grant the minister the gifts necessary for service. But the great promise of Scripture is that God does call ministers, and presents these servants as gifts to the church.

One key issue here is a common misunderstanding about the will of God. Some models of evangelical piety imply that God's will is something difficult for us to accept. We sometimes confuse this further by talking about "surrendering" to the will of God. As Paul makes clear in Romans 12:2, the will of God is good, worthy of eager acceptance, and perfect. Those called by God to preach will be given a desire to preach, as well as the gifts of preaching. Beyond this, the God-called preacher will feel the same compulsion as the great apostle, who wrote, "Woe to me if I do not preach the gospel!" (1 Corinthians 9:16 ESV).

Foreword

Consider your calling. Do you sense that God is calling you to ministry, whether as pastor or another servant of the church? Do you burn with a compulsion to proclaim the word, share the gospel, and care for God's flock? Has this call been confirmed and encouraged by those Christians who know you best?

In this new and important book, Brian Croft presents a bold and biblical understanding of the call to ministry. Along the way, Brian clarifies many issues of contemporary confusion, and his commitment to the local church ensures that his understanding of the call to ministry is never severed from the context of God's people.

Few books are timelier than this one, and I am thankful to Brian Croft for his faithful and careful consideration of the call to ministry

R. Albert Mohler Jr., president of
The Southern Baptist Theological Seminary

INTRODUCTION

A GREAT NEED EMERGED EARLY in my pastoral ministry. The church I was serving saw steady growth in the first few years, including attracting several students from a local seminary. As I built relationships with these young men pursuing pastoral ministry, I found they had many wonderful qualities. Each one of them loved God. Their lives had been transformed by the gospel. They loved the local church. They each felt the call of God to pursue full-time occupational ministry. And each one had made the decision to enroll in seminary with the expectation that they would be trained and equipped for the work of pastoral ministry.

As I grew to know these young men, however, there were also some common elements to their stories that concerned me. Most had come to seminary without any kind of corporate affirmation from a local church. Like most seminaries, the school they attended required an affirmation of calling from a local church as part of the admission process. Yet, after some investigating, I learned that in most cases their church affirmation amounted to little more than a letter of approval for them to attend the school. None of them had experienced a corporate affirmation of their gifts for the ministry. None of them had been tested or trained by a local church. They had permission to attend, but not affirmation and support from the local body of believers.

Prepare Them to Shepherd

I also discovered that these students expected the seminary would take up this responsibility for them, helping to affirm and prepare them for the challenges and struggles of ministry. But as Albert Mohler, president of The Southern Baptist Theological Seminary, has stated on more than one occasion, this is not the role or responsibility of a seminary:

> I emphatically believe that the best and most proper place for the education and preparation of pastors is in the local church. We should be ashamed that churches fail miserably in their responsibility to train future pastors. Established pastors should be ashamed if they are not pouring themselves into the lives of young men whom God has called into the teaching and leadership ministry of the church.[1]

In other words, seminaries do not and should not see themselves as the ones responsible for selecting, testing, and affirming ministerial callings. They see this, rightfully, as the role and responsibility of the local church. So if seminaries expect local churches to do this, and if local churches (and students) are presuming that seminaries are taking the reins, who is truly responsible — and ultimately accountable to God — for all of this? The failure to answer these essential questions has placed unnecessary pressure on seminaries and Bible colleges, has led to widespread confusion among those seeking a pastoral calling for ministry, and has allowed the local church to neglect her divine mandate to prepare the next generation of shepherds for God's flock.

There is arguably no better work on the responsibility and the process for assessing God's calling than the writings of

Introduction

Charles Bridges (1794 – 1869). In his book *The Christian Ministry*, Bridges places the responsibility for the determination of one's call on both the conscience of the individual and the local church to which he is committed. Bridges refers to these two aspects of calling as the internal and the external call of God:

> *The external call* is a commission received from and recognized by the Church … not indeed qualifying the Minister, but accrediting him, whom God had internally and suitably qualified. This call communicates therefore only official authority. *The internal call* is the voice and power of the Holy Ghost, directing the will and the judgment, and conveying personal qualifications. Both calls, however — though essentially distinct in their character and source — are indispensable for the exercise of our commission.[2]

Bridges says that an individual must receive an internal call to know he is truly called by God to serve in the ministry. This is a God-given desire to do the work of the ministry, combined with his own conviction that he has been gifted and empowered by God's Spirit to do this work.

In addition to the internal call, however, an individual must also possess an external call. This is the affirmation from a local church that he possesses the gifts and godly character suitable for a Christian minister. Bridges, Charles Spurgeon, and many other godly men, whom God used in the past to prepare those called into the ministry, all agree that both the internal and external calls are necessary for a person to enter into the work of the ministry.

Unfortunately, few today experience this sort of dual calling. Over the last century, the role of the local church and the importance of the external call have diminished, and one could argue that even the need for an internal call is less important today as people treat pastoral ministry as just one career option among many. A recovery of the biblical teaching on these matters is urgently needed—and that is the reason I've written this short book.

As you'll see in the pages that follow, the Bible clearly reveals that both the internal and external call should be centered and grounded in God's design and his purposes for his people. God has given the responsibility for making an external calling to his church, and he has given specific requirements as to who should receive it. In addition to looking at the responsibility and requirements for making a call, we will also look at how a local church fulfills the role of training and preparing people—and what is at stake if a church neglects to do this. Since there is often confusion about this, the subtitles for each chapter have been formatted as questions to help the reader.

The goal of this book, then, is to challenge your vision of local church ministry and to change the way individuals are prepared, trained, tested, and sent into ministry today. God's calling for each of us is to be a follower of Christ. This common calling should inspire us to service and ministry in the body of Christ. But we must also seek to be faithful in examining the calling that God places on individuals to lead, teach, and care for his people in the local church as pastors, seeking how best to prepare and equip them to serve on the front lines of his glorious and eternal kingdom work on earth.

CHAPTER 1

CALLING
To What Is a Pastor Called?

> To the elders among you, I appeal as a fellow elder and a witness of Christ's sufferings who also will share in the glory to be revealed: Be shepherds of God's flock that is under your care ... And when the Chief Shepherd appears, you will receive the crown of glory that will never fade away.
>
> 1 Peter 5:1–2, 4

IN LATER CHAPTERS we will look at questions about who receives the external call to pastor, how that call happens, and who carries it out. But as we begin, it seems appropriate to start with God's intention and design for the care of his people. We want to know what, exactly, is the nature of the work to which a pastor is called? How does pastoral ministry fit in with God's larger purpose in caring for his people?

The aim of this first chapter is to examine what the Bible teaches about God's design for the care of his people and how God calls some to minister that care to others in the body of Christ. God's purposes are evident from the very beginning, and they run throughout the narrative of Scripture. The story line of the Bible evidences God's design for the church through a key theme: God's appointed leaders are called to instruct, care for, and shepherd God's people under God's authority.

One of the most helpful ways to understand how God cares for his people is through the biblical image of God as a shepherd. Some today suggest it is unhelpful or culturally irrelevant to think of God's care for his people using this shepherding imagery. A well-known pastor of one of the largest churches in America was once asked if we should stop referring to pastors as "shepherds." He responded:

> That word [*shepherd*] needs to go away. Jesus talked about shepherds because there was one over there in a pasture he could point to. But to bring in that imagery today and say, "Pastor, you're the shepherd of the flock," no. I've never seen a flock. I've never spent five minutes with a shepherd. It was culturally relevant in the time of Jesus, but it's not culturally relevant anymore.
>
> Nothing works in our culture with that model except this sense of the gentle, pastoral care. Obviously that is a face of church ministry, but that's not leadership.[3]

So is there merit to this critique? Is this image of God's care as a shepherd caring for sheep unnecessary today, perhaps outdated? Is it an unhelpful picture on which to model our own leadership of God's people? On the contrary, I would argue that it is difficult to accurately grasp the biblical understanding of pastoral ministry if we fail to understand how God is a *shepherd* to his own people. This image, more than any other, captures the essence of the role to which God calls those we commonly refer to as "pastors." Church leadership, before it is anything else then, is about *shepherding* people.

Creation

The Bible begins its historical narrative with a picture of a world that is foreign to us today. God created the heavens, the earth, and all living creatures (Genesis 1 – 2). He also created man and woman in his image (Genesis 1:27) and saw all that he had made was very good (Genesis 1:31). He placed the man and woman in the Garden of Eden, where they are to rule over his creation and be fruitful and multiply. The garden was beautiful, and in it there flowed a river to water the garden and the tree of life that was good for food (Genesis 2:9 – 10). This world was perfectly made. Man was created in the image of God; man enjoyed unhindered fellowship with God; and man ruled over the creation while fully submitting to God's rule over him.

As a result, man also enjoyed the unhindered care, leadership, and authority of God in his life. God perfectly led man, and man perfectly followed. Man trusted in God's goodness, care, and provision and did not resent the authority that the Creator exercised over the creation.

Fall

Yet this world we find in Genesis 1 – 2 is not the world we live in today. The reality of life is that something is now wrong with the world and with those who are made in God's image. The reason behind this familiar understanding of the world we see today can be found in Genesis 3, where we learn that Adam and Eve sinned by disobeying God's word when they ate from the tree of the knowledge of good and evil (Genesis 3:6). God told them not to eat from this tree or they would die (Genesis 2:17). Satan tempted Eve, and she ate from the tree and gave some of its fruit to her husband (Genesis 3:6). Instead of obeying God's command, they rebelled against him. The first man and woman wanted to rule, not be ruled by God.

As a result of their sin, the curse of death that God warned them about did indeed come on them, affecting all of God's creation. On that day, sin—with all of its ramifications—entered the world. Adam and Eve were removed from the garden and barred from access to the tree of life, whose fruit would grant eternal life (Genesis 3:22). Pain and difficulty would now mar life, from childbirth to daily labor (Genesis 3:16). A great separation from their once unhindered fellowship with God now existed. Most significantly, death entered the world with sin and affected all of creation. As a result, man would suffer not just death but also the effects of death—old age, pain, and suffering.

Another significant ramification of man's separation from God is that God no longer led, cared for, and shepherded man as he had before the fall. Instead of submitting to God, man rebelled against his authority, rejecting the loving care of his Creator and straying from the flock of the good shepherd. Starting from this place of hopelessness and despair in the story line of the Bible, we see our desperate need for redemption. Immediately, it is revealed to man and woman (and to us) that only a sovereign, eternal God can intervene to save creation from the curse of sin and death. The hope of the gospel includes this promise of restored and unhindered fellowship with the Chief Shepherd, and from the very first pages of Scripture it begins to unfold in a glorious work of redemption that will ultimately culminate in Jesus' life, death, and resurrection.

The Life of Israel

The first part of God's plan to redeem mankind comes about through a chosen nation that is selected to be God's own people, unique among all the other nations of the earth. This nation was promised to a man named Abraham (Genesis 12) through his son, Isaac (Genesis 21). From Isaac came Jacob, who would later be called Israel. And through Jacob's twelve sons and their descendants, we see the formation of the nation of Israel and the beginning of the fulfillment of God's promises to Abraham. One of Jacob's sons, Joseph, eventually led his family and the future nation of Israel to safety in Egypt during a time of famine, and during the centuries that followed, the people multiplied in number (Exodus 1:7). Eventually, they also became enslaved to the Egyptians. This was not a surprise to God, as he had promised hundreds of years before this (Genesis 15:13–14) that he would deliver his people from their oppression and judge the nation that held them captive. Through the events of their deliverance from Egypt, God appointed a man named Moses, who would lead, care for, and shepherd God's people.

Like many whom God divinely appoints to lead and care for his people, Moses felt inadequately equipped for his calling. During Moses' burning bush experience, God calls Moses to deliver his enslaved people (Exodus 3:10). Moses (on several occasions) tries to wiggle out of his calling. Moses argues with God, telling him he is unable to execute the task given to him (Exodus 3:11; 4:1, 10). We see in God's response to Moses a pattern that will be repeated time after time in the story of the Bible. Whenever God calls a leader out for his people, that leader is found to be weak and inadequate. Yet God provides empowerment to the leader to carry out the calling. In the case of Moses, God gives him the power, the words, and the ability to be faithful to his call to lead and shepherd God's people. What is the point of this repeated theme? It is intended to help us see that even when God uses men to lead, it is ultimately God himself who leads. God leads his people through the one he appoints. That leader does not have the authority to act independently of God.

God gives Moses his blessing and tells him to present himself before Pharaoh and the people of Israel in the name of YHWH, the great I AM (Exodus 3:14). God gives Moses the power to perform signs and wonders, signs that point to God—affirming that God is indeed with Moses (Exodus 4:1–5). God even helps by speaking on behalf of Moses when he lacks the words (Exodus 4:10–12). When God appoints a man to lead, care for, and shepherd his people, he promises to work through him to care for his people and accomplish his purposes.

In the example of Moses, we also learn there are devastating consequences when the one who leads God's people fails. Though Moses delivers the people through God's guidance and power, leads them to make a covenant with God, and journeys up the mountain to retrieve God's law for the people, in his absence the people turn away and rebel. While Moses is absent, his brother Aaron fails to lead faithfully, giving in to pressure from the people (Exodus 32:1). Gross idolatry and rebellion are the result (Exodus 32:1 – 10). From this we see the dire consequences of failed leadership. When the shepherd fails to lead, the sheep are easily led astray.

We see further evidence of God's faithful provision in spite of the failure of human leadership as the Israelite monarchy is established. Though Israel was God's chosen people with God as their King, in their disobedience and sin they cried out to God for another king, a human king who would lead them like the other nations (1 Samuel 8:5). Though this desire was a rejection of God's leadership (1 Samuel 8:8), God allowed them to have a king, while warning them of the disaster that would follow. As the story unfolds, we see that everything the Lord warns them about does indeed come to pass when Saul becomes the first king of Israel (1 Samuel 8:10 – 22). The reign of King Saul brings heartache, tragedy, and disobedience that ultimately lead to great suffering for God's people. Yet in God's mercy he selects another king (1 Samuel 16:1), who, despite his imperfections, rules in righteousness, justice, and humility before the Lord. King David, like Moses, was also a shepherd. David is also described as a man after God's own heart (Acts 13:22). God appoints David to care for his people and to rule them as a shepherd-king, leading and caring for God's people on God's behalf. Even more significantly, it is through David's descendants that the Messiah — God's eternal Redeemer, Shepherd, and King —

finally comes, redeeming people from the curse of sin and death (2 Samuel 7).

After a long series of failed kings following David, Israel enters a period of exile. During this time the prophets develop an expectation that a future king, the Messiah, will come and restore the nation to freedom and righteousness. The prophets are not hesitant to point out the flaws and failures among Israel's leaders, repeatedly accusing them of being unfaithful and negligent shepherds of God's people. The prophets Jeremiah, Zechariah, and Ezekiel all warn these unfaithful shepherds about the consequences of their neglect:

> "Woe to the shepherds who are destroying and scattering the sheep of my pasture!" declares the LORD. Therefore this is what the LORD, the God of Israel, says to the shepherds who tend my people: "Because you have scattered my flock and driven them away and have not bestowed care on them, I will bestow punishment on you for the evil you have done," declares the LORD.
>
> Jeremiah 23:1–2

An unfaithful shepherd harms the flock of God by his neglect, bringing ultimate judgment on himself. Still, God does not abandon his people. Even in the midst of these unfaithful shepherds, God appoints a shepherd who will faithfully lead and care for his people.

The appointed shepherd, who points us to the good shepherd and redeemer yet to come, is the prophet Zechariah. In the absence of faithful shepherds, God calls Zechariah to lead his people. But Zechariah is not accepted as a leader; he is rejected by the people.

Calling

"Awake, sword, against my shepherd,
    against the man who is close to me!"
    declares the LORD Almighty.
"Strike the shepherd,
    and the sheep will be scattered."

Zechariah 13:7

Zechariah's rejection and suffering as God's leader points us to the future good shepherd who will also suffer to redeem his people. The word of the prophet concludes with God's people scattered, living in disobedience and discouragement, yet holding tight to the promised hope of a redeemer—the good shepherd to come (Ezekiel 34:23). Despite the repeated unfaithfulness of the people and the failures of their leaders, God is faithful to the covenant he has made.

The Life of Christ

After many years of silence, God breaks through the despair and suffering of his people with a voice—a man calling in the wilderness to prepare the way for the Lord (Mark 1:3). The voice belongs to John the Baptist, the forerunner who comes to prepare others for the redeemer. All four gospels identify Jesus as this redeemer, the long-awaited Messiah who saves his people from their sins and ushers in the kingdom of God. Mark points us to Jesus Christ as this redeemer in Jesus' first recorded words of his gospel account: "The time has come ... The kingdom of God has come near. Repent and believe the good news" (Mark 1:15). The kingdom has arrived in the person of Jesus.

Jesus comes in the authority of God as the Son of God (Mark 1:1). His authority is seen by his power over sickness, demons, and death. Jesus also reveals his authority as ruler over God's kingdom when he claims the title of shepherd over God's people. John affirms this claim when he records these words from Jesus: "I am the good shepherd; I know my sheep and my sheep know me—just as the Father knows me and I know the Father—and I lay down my life for the sheep" (John 10:14–15).

Jesus proves to be the long-awaited good shepherd who suffers for God's people by laying down his life for the sheep, thus fulfilling the words of the prophet Zechariah. Jesus eats his final Passover meal with his disciples, and the next recorded words of Jesus are identical to the words written by the prophet: "You will all fall away ... for it is written: 'I will strike the shepherd, and the sheep will be scattered'" (Mark 14:27). Zechariah spoke these words as an indictment against the unfaithful shepherds of Israel, but Jesus speaks them in reference to himself, pointing us to his perfect faithfulness as a good shepherd who willingly lays down his life for his sheep. With the striking of the shepherd, his followers are scattered for a short time, until he is reunited with them after his resurrection (Mark 14:28).

Following his resurrection, Jesus spoke of the authority that is now eternally his as the ruler of God's kingdom: "All authority in heaven and on earth has been given to me. Therefore go and make disciples of all nations, baptizing them in the name of the Father and of the Son and of the Holy Spirit, and teaching them to obey everything I have commanded you. And surely I am with you always, to the very end of the age" (Matthew 28:18–20). As the good shepherd, with authority given to him by God, Jesus now commands his disciples to go and gather his sheep from among the nations.

The Life of the Church

Jesus died, rose from the dead, and appeared to many witnesses until he ascended to be with the Father. Following his ascension, Jesus empowered his disciples through the gift of the Holy Spirit, empowering them to lead, care for, and shepherd his people. The church is birthed at Pentecost (Acts 2), and the apostles go out to be Christ's witnesses to the world (Acts 1:8).

As the early church grows, the leadership structure develops as well. In the structure of the church, revealed to the apostles and recorded in Scripture, we see further evidence of exactly how the good shepherd (Jesus) will continue his care for his sheep. The apostles are the first to be appointed by God to lead and shepherd his people under Christ's authority. This transfer of authority from Jesus to his apostles is seen in Jesus' conversation with Peter. John records that Jesus asked Peter three times if he loved him. Each time, Peter answers saying, "Yes, Lord, you know that I love you." Jesus responds to Peter by telling him to feed and to take care of Jesus' sheep (John 21:15 – 17). This same apostolic authority is also given to Paul when he is radically converted on the Damascus road (Acts 9:3 – 6) and appointed by Christ to be the apostle to the Gentiles (Acts 9:15 – 16). Through these apostles, the early church leadership structure is established, and the responsibilities and roles of those who lead, care for, and shepherd God's people are clarified. As we will see, many of the responsibilities for leadership and care are passed down from the apostles to those called to be pastors — God's shepherd-leaders in the church.

Prepare Them to Shepherd

The earliest picture of this type of pastoral leadership is found in the book of Acts. In Acts 6 we see that the responsibility to lead, care for, and shepherd God's people is divided into several specific roles. There are those who will wait on tables (verse 2) and those who will be devoted to prayer and the ministry of the word (verse 4). The apostle Paul further develops our understanding of leadership in the early church when he writes to Timothy and describes the qualifications for a pastor[4]—the name he gives to the biblical office that is responsible to lead, care for, and shepherd God's people within the local church (1 Timothy 3:1–7). Paul also writes to Titus, urging him to appoint elders (pastors) in every city (Titus 1:5). Through these examples and the writings of Paul, we see that the tasks and responsibilities of leadership are passed from the apostles to local church pastors. These men are now appointed by God and empowered by the Holy Spirit to shepherd Christ's sheep. Peter gives a wonderfully clear description of this role when he writes in his first letter:

> To the elders among you, I appeal as a fellow elder and a witness of Christ's sufferings who also will share in the glory to be revealed: Be shepherds of God's flock that is under your care, watching over them—not because you must, but because you are willing, as God wants you to be; not pursuing dishonest gain, but eager to serve; not lording it over those entrusted to you, but being examples to the flock. And when the Chief Shepherd appears, you will receive the crown of glory that will never fade away.
>
> 1 Peter 5:1–4

In what Peter writes, we notice that a number of shepherds are appointed—not just one. We also notice the manner in which they shepherd—voluntarily, eagerly, and exemplarily. And we see to whom they are ultimately accountable—the Chief Shepherd, Jesus Christ. Though the task of leadership and care has passed from the apostles, God does not abandon his people. He establishes pastors—shepherds who will lead and care for his people until the Chief Shepherd returns for his church and consummates his kingdom rule.

New Creation

The unfolding of God's redemptive plan for all creation will come to an end someday. The final destination for those who follow Christ is not a disembodied existence of life after death. When Jesus returns, he will come for his bride, judge the nations, punish the wicked, and fully consummate his kingdom in the new heaven and new earth. This state is known as the new creation, and it is one in which the curse of sin is fully and permanently reversed. God's kingdom people will not just experience a physical resurrection; they will know eternal fellowship with Jesus our Savior, King, and Shepherd.

In this new creation, God will restore his role as the good shepherd to his people through Jesus, who is the one appointed by God to shepherd. John gives us a powerful picture of this restored relationship:

> Then one of the elders asked me, "These in white robes—who are they, and where did they come from?"
>
> I answered, "Sir, you know."
>
> And he said, "These are they who have come out of the great tribulation; they have washed their robes and made them white in the blood of the Lamb. Therefore,

"they are before the throne of God
> and serve him day and night in his temple;
and he who sits on the throne
> will shelter them with his presence.
'Never again will they hunger;
> never again will they thirst.
The sun will not beat down on them,'
> nor any scorching heat.
For the Lamb at the center of the throne
> *will be their shepherd*;
'he will lead them to springs of living water.'
> 'And God will wipe away every tear from their eyes.'"

Revelation 7:13–17, emphasis added

John tells us that Christ came as the Lamb of God to be slaughtered on behalf of his people, and he will now be the eternal shepherd to God's people. The Lamb becomes the shepherd, and he restores through his sacrifice what was lost in the fall. The image of Jesus as a shepherd is not outdated—it is essential to understanding the future! Knowing what it means to shepherd people is a key element for perceiving how Christ will relate to his people in the kingdom yet to come.

The unfolding story line of the Bible helps us grasp God's plan for his people as we see how he leads and cares for them in this fallen world as they await Christ's return. This understanding is foundational for perceiving the purpose of a pastor in a local church. So how do we recognize, affirm, and place the right people—those called by God—into this role? What is involved in appointing shepherds to pastor the church? The next chapter will answer this question.

CHAPTER 2

ACCOUNTABILITY
Who Is Responsible for the Call?

> I emphatically believe that the best and
> most proper place for the education and
> preparation of pastors is in the local church.
>
> R. Albert Mohler Jr.

WHO IS RESPONSIBLE FOR CALLING someone into ministry? Who has the God-given authority to do so? Is it the responsibility of a seminary or Bible college? Can a mission organization or parachurch ministry issue such a call? Or perhaps it is the responsibility of denominational leaders, or even the close friends of an individual? Sadly, the responsibility for the training and affirming of an individual's call often gets passively handed over to whoever is willing to do it. So before we look at who is responsible, let's look at who is not responsible.

Unmerited Responsibility

For over a century, most of the training a person received for pastoral ministry was done by seminaries and Bible colleges. These organizations have some of the most brilliant scholars in theology, church history, hermeneutics, and the original biblical languages. In addition, the faculty typically contains gifted pastors who bring decades of pastoral experience to the classroom. These academic settings hold students to a rigorous standard of reading, studying, and theological engagement—a level that few have the personal discipline to achieve on their own. Yet as important as theological education is in preparation for a call, God has not given these institutions the responsibility or the authority to issue or affirm a call.

What about mission organizations or parachurch ministries? Many of the pioneering missionary efforts of the past two hundred years began because churches and denominations could not or would not support sending missionaries to dangerous, hard-to-reach places. The great Scottish Presbyterian missionary John Paton took the gospel to the New Hebrides Islands in the mid-nineteenth century. But he had very little support from the church or from his fellow Christians. Paton recalls an older Christian who tried to discourage him from following his call to evangelize pagan lands by warning him, "You will be eaten by cannibals!"[5]

Because they lacked support from the majority of the church, missionaries of the eighteenth and nineteenth centuries turned to nonecclesial structures, forming missionary committees and other sending organizations. And God has greatly used these organizations to bring the gospel to the nations. The missionary efforts of the International Mission Board, the China Inland Mission, the Voice of the Martyrs, To Every Tribe Ministries, and many others have been used by God to bring millions to saving faith. So is the missionary board or a missions organization responsible for calling and confirming a person into ministry? Indeed, the Bible reveals a different norm, placing the responsibility elsewhere.

We might also consider parachurch and denominational ministries. For younger generations, these kinds of ministries sometimes fill a void, replacing the role of a local church. If you were to spend some time on a typical college campus and attend the evening gathering of the Baptist Student Union, Campus Crusade for Christ, or the Fellowship of Christian Athletes, you would find professing Christians, faithful attendees, and even those sensing a call into the ministry who have no further Christian affiliation — nor do they sense a need for one — apart from the parachurch organization to which they belong. In addition, many of the staff positions of these ministries are filled by those who have come up through the ranks, having been trained solely within the organization. Though there are occasional exceptions — times when a Christian in a local church may sense a call into a specialized ministry — most of those who belong to these organizations see them as their primary community for training and fellowship. Still, regardless of the effectiveness or fruitfulness of a particular ministry, it does not change the reality that God has appointed a different strategy for the testing, training, affirming, and sending of those he calls.

Finally, there are times when individual Christians, especially those who know a person well, offer affirmation and encouragement to a person, telling him to attend seminary or suggesting that he should be a pastor. These are typically people who have had a significant influence on the individual throughout his life. Perhaps they knew him when he was a boy or before he was a Christian. Or they once taught his Sunday school class. Maybe they prayed with him when he surrendered his life to God to pursue the ministry. Of all the potentially responsible parties, it would seem most natural that these people are best equipped to assess the character and qualifications of the individual and validate or affirm his calling to ministry. Yet as helpful as these credible witnesses are in guiding a brother to pursue the call of God, God has not given them the responsibility to issue the call. He has a different solution.

To be clear, God has mightily used seminaries, mission organizations, parachurch ministries, and individual Christians to equip the called and build God's kingdom powerfully throughout the centuries. There is no question that these institutions and individuals have furthered the gospel and helped make disciples. Yet the key question we need to ask is not what has worked or what seems natural. We need to ask who has been biblically commissioned by God to take ultimate responsibility for testing, training, affirming, and sending those who are called to be pastors and missionaries. So who is ultimately responsible? The local church.

The Local Church

It should come as no surprise that the local church is the community appointed by God to bear this responsibility, a call that has belonged to the church from the very beginning. In Acts 13 we get a glimpse of this at the church in Antioch. From this example, we can learn how a local church should understand the role and function of the external call. Luke recounts the calling of Saul and Barnabas as they prepare to be sent on their first missionary journey. Here is the scene he describes:

> Now in the church at Antioch there were prophets and teachers: Barnabas, Simeon called Niger, Lucius of Cyrene, Manaen (who had been brought up with Herod the tetrarch) and Saul. While they were worshiping the Lord and fasting, the Holy Spirit said, "Set apart for me Barnabas and Saul for the work to which I have called them." So after they had fasted and prayed, they placed their hands on them and sent them off.
>
> Acts 13:1–3

We see several truths about the external call in this short passage. First, the responsibility for giving the external call is centered in the local church. There are no special groups or mission organizations present to make this call. Certainly, specialized organizations can be helpful in the process of clarifying and refining a call; nevertheless, we must remember that these organizations have developed over time for various reasons. They can certainly assist the church in fulfilling its responsibility, but they should never usurp the role of the church as described in the Scriptures. Again, testing, training, affirming, and sending pastors and missionaries is the *sole responsibility of the local church.* James Montgomery Boice writes of the church of Antioch, "God does what he does through tools, and in the case of missionary work the tool God uses is his church. At Antioch we have an example of a mighty missionary tool, a church that was established, well-taught, integrated, active, and seeking God's direction."[6]

We see in this passage that the prophets and teachers (Acts 13:1) were the leaders of the early church. They were the primary means through which God revealed his will for Saul and Barnabas. Saul and Barnabas were first recognized by the pastors. These leaders were likely engaging in their normal routine. Luke tells us they were worshiping the Lord and fasting (verse 2) — in other words, they were doing the work of the church by preaching and teaching God's word, shepherding the church, and being deliberately prayerful about it. Fasting is the purposeful setting aside of eating to concentrate on spiritual issues, predominantly through times of focused prayer. Through the faithful, regular ministry of these leaders, the Holy Spirit revealed God's will for Saul and Barnabas. They were to be "set apart" for God — for the work to which he had "called them" (verse 2).

Consider for a moment the way God revealed his guidance in this situation. First and foremost, the leaders had certainty that the message they received was from the Holy Spirit (Acts 13:2). But in addition to this clear and unanimous sense, they were aware of the fruitfulness of Saul's and Barnabas's previous labor. At the end of Acts 11, Saul and Barnabas arrive at the church at Antioch and spend an entire year (verse 26) in fellowship, living in community with the church, meeting together, and caring for the members. The church and its leaders had certainty of God's call because they had already witnessed the fruitfulness of these men's past labor among them. They were able to affirm them, not only by God's guidance through his Spirit, but by their own experience in serving and ministering alongside Saul and Barnabas. As they sought the wisdom of God through continual fasting and praying, they sensed God's call and laid their hands on these two men to affirm them in the call (Acts 13:3).

The affirmation of these prophets and teachers as representative leaders is an extension of the entire church in calling these men to ministry (Acts 6:5 – 6; 14:27). Since the Antioch church and its leaders have been able to see the ministry of Saul and Barnabas with their own eyes, and they have sought the Lord's guidance, they now officially apply the external call of God on Saul and Barnabas by laying their hands on them in affirmation (Acts 13:3). Through the laying on of hands they "sent them off" (verse 3). We see that the Spirit worked through the church as the church affirms and sends them (verse 3), but Luke is clear in telling us that Saul and Barnabas are also sent by the Spirit directly (verse 4). In other words, this is a work done by the church, but it is also a work of God. When Saul and Barnabas return to report, they "gathered the church together and reported all that God had done through them" (Acts 14:27). Through the Holy Spirit, the leaders (prophets and teachers) and the church have a central role in the process of calling Saul and Barnabas to the work to which God had called them. This is how God builds his church and brings the gospel to the world — by working through the church and its leaders.

Though this example in Acts focuses on the importance of affirming and sending out missionaries, supporting texts throughout the New Testament suggest this same process applies to any who are called into the gospel ministry. Paul later writes to Titus, a church leader, and instructs him to "appoint elders in every town" (Titus 1:5). Paul also writes to Timothy, "And the things you have heard me say in the presence of many witnesses entrust to reliable people who will also be qualified to teach others" (2 Timothy 2:2). We see the scene in Acts 13 repeated in Timothy's own pastoral calling when Paul refers to other pastors laying hands on Timothy in affirmation of his gifts and calling (1 Timothy 4:14). Regardless of the type of gospel ministry, the Bible is clear. The identification, affirmation, and sending of pastors and missionaries is the responsibility of the leaders of the local church.

A Convenient Ambiguity

Though there are clear truths we can observe in this scene from Acts 13, there is also a convenient ambiguity in the outworking of this process. Though the process is evident — recognition of gifts, guidance through the Spirit, affirmation and sending by the local church — the process can be applied faithfully in a variety of diverse contexts. This should unite local churches in embracing their common call, even if there are differences in structure or polity.

For example, an elder-led congregational church, an elder-ruled church, a single pastor/staff-led church, or even a deacon-led church can all read Acts 13:1 – 3 and affirm that they are responsible for the external call. In the outworking of this process to test, train, affirm, and send within their particular context and structure, there may be some differences. The account in Acts shows us that the local church was God's instrument for calling Saul and Barnabas, that the leaders of the church led in this process, and that the congregation was involved to some degree in these men's lives to affirm and send them. Where the balance of authority lands and how roles are distributed within the local church will depend on the structure of the church. Though we each have a particular conviction regarding the structure of polity, nevertheless, this ambiguity exists. We may disagree on polity while agreeing on the need for local churches to reclaim their responsibility for the external call.

God has called out a people for salvation from every nation, tribe, people, and language to build his kingdom and to display his glory to the nations. Though God uses many diverse people and organizations to accomplish his purposes, the authority and responsibility for building God's kingdom and displaying his glory rest solely on God's redeemed people within the context of the local church. God has divinely ordained the local church to grant the external call to an individual seeking the call of God. May our local churches and our leaders be awakened to feel the weight of this responsibility — for the sake of those called and for the further ministry of the gospel in the world.

CHAPTER 3

QUALIFICATION
Who Should Receive the Call?

> It need scarcely be said that piety is essential. No amount of talent, no extent of education, no apparent brilliancy of fervor, should even be allowed to gain admission into the ministry for one whose piety there is a reason to doubt, or who has not a more than ordinary active and consistent holiness.
>
> Basil Manly Jr., "A Call to the Ministry"

WE HAVE LOOKED AT WHO IS RESPONSIBLE for giving the external call, but now we must ask, "Who should receive the external call?" A church needs to think through this question biblically before acting to confer its blessing on just anyone who wants to pursue ministry. Sadly, many churches today base their external call on nothing more than an individual's sense of internal "calling"—his own subjective perception. If a man has the desire to do the work of the ministry and seems gifted, the church assumes he is called. To be sure, a man's own assessment is important. Nonetheless, the church cannot rely on a subjective assessment or an unfalsifiable feeling in the man himself. They need a tangible process that tests a man's qualifications for ministry against those laid out in Scripture.

The aim of this chapter is to look at what the Bible reveals about the process for assessing who should receive this external call from the local church. We will also consider how pastors and theologians throughout church history have evaluated men who believe they are sensing an internal calling from God. In looking at this process, saints from both the past and present have offered four answers based on the biblical qualifications for pastors found in 1 Timothy 3:1 – 7.[7]

A Christian Man Transformed by the Gospel of Jesus Christ

A man who senses an internal call to enter the sacred office of a minister of the gospel must first be transformed by the gospel. The gospel is the message of salvation from sin and from God's wrath. It declares that a sinner receives salvation by grace through repentance of sin and faith in the person and work of Jesus Christ. It may seem obvious that a man entering the ministry should himself have saving faith in Christ. Yet this qualification has, time after time, been a legitimate concern. In the seventeenth century, for example, Richard Baxter began his celebrated book *The Reformed Pastor* this way:

> Take heed to yourselves, lest you be void of that saving grace of God which you offer to others, and be strangers to the effectual working of that gospel which you preach; and lest, while you proclaim to the world the necessity of a Savior, your own hearts should neglect him and you should miss of an interest in him and his saving benefits.

41

Take heed to yourselves, lest you perish, while you call upon others to take heed of perishing; and lest you famish yourselves while you prepare food for them ... Many have warned others that they come not to that place of torment, while yet they hastened to it themselves; many a preacher is now in hell, who hath a hundred times called upon his hearers to use the utmost care and diligence to escape it.[8]

Baxter's warning should continue to resonate with us today in the twenty-first century. Much is at stake if local churches neglect the importance of carefully evaluating candidates for pastoral ministry. If a man is still in darkness, enslaved to sin, and living in rebellion against God, he should not be placed in a position where he is entrusted with the gospel and the responsibility of shepherding redeemed souls.

A Christian Man Who Desires This Fine Work

The apostle Paul instructs his young protégé, "Here is a trustworthy saying: Whoever aspires to be an overseer [pastor] desires a noble task" (1 Timothy 3:1). The great nineteenth-century Baptist Charles Spurgeon lectured young men preparing for the ministry, "The first sign of the heavenly calling is an intense, all-absorbing desire for the work."[9] There should be a strong, unquenchable desire in a man to do the work of a pastor. He should have a desire to preach God's word, shepherd God's people, evangelize the lost, disciple the spiritually immature, and serve the local church.

Spurgeon confirms that this divine aspiration that comes from above can be known through a desire to do nothing else:

Qualification

If any student in this room could be content to be a newspaper editor, or a grocer, or a farmer or a doctor, or a lawyer, or a senator, or a king, in the name of heaven and earth let him go his way; he is not the man in whom dwells the Spirit of God in its fulness, for a man so filled with God would utterly weary of any pursuit but that for which his inmost soul pants. If on the other hand, you can say that for all the wealth of both the Indies you could not and dare not espouse any other calling so as to be put aside from preaching the gospel of Jesus Christ, then, depend upon it, if other things be equally satisfactory, you have the signs of this apostleship. We must feel that woe is unto us if we preach not the gospel; the word of God must be unto us as fire in our bones, otherwise, if we undertake the ministry, we shall be unhappy in it, shall be unable to bear the self-denials incident to it, and shall be of little service to those among whom we minister.[10]

Why is an unquenchable longing for this work required? Because the work of ministry is not for the faint of heart. It is a work fraught with struggles, challenges, discouragements, pressures, and spiritual battles that can cripple the strongest of men who have an "ordinary" desire for the work. It should be, instead, a desire that cannot be stolen when your brother betrays you, a desire that cannot be weakened when your job is threatened, a desire that cannot be quenched when physical, mental, and emotional fatigue firmly take root. And it is a desire that should increase over time. Basil Manly Jr., a nineteenth-century Baptist minister and educator, writes of this increasing desire for the work:

This steadfast and divinely implanted desire to labor for souls is substantially what is meant by "the internal call." It may be distinguished from the early zeal, which young converts usually have, and which generally subsides into a calm principle of benevolent activity in their own particular sphere. In the man truly called, it grows, it increases. As he reflects on it, and prays about it, the great salvation becomes greater and nearer to him than when he first believed; the guilt and ruin of immortal souls weigh heavily upon him; he feels impelled to warn them to flee the wrath to come.

Sometimes the thought presses on one, so that he cannot rest. The strongest promptings of self-interest, the greatest timidity and natural reserve, the most violent opposition of irreligious relatives and influential friends, and even the most serious peril, prove insufficient to check this holy ardor. The man is made to feel that for him all other avocations are trifling, all worldly employments unattractive. "Woe is me," he cries, "if I preach not the Gospel!" Jails, and fetters, and the stake, have no terrors for him comparable with the guilt of disobeying Jesus, and the frown of his redeemer.[11]

A Christian man who has an "irresistible, overwhelming craving and raging thirst" for this fine work should receive the external call.[12]

A Christian Man Whose Character and Life Qualify Biblically

Many faithful, godly men throughout the ages have displayed Christ in their character and have modeled sacrificial service to his church. Yet not all have been called to the work of pastor/elder. Paul writes to Timothy and gives a separate list of qualifications for the office of pastor/elder, distinct from that of deacons (1 Timothy 3:8–13). This list demonstrates that there is a unique calling and work that a pastor is set apart to do. These qualifications provide a way for others to evaluate externally and objectively a man who claims to have a desire for this work. Paul's list of qualifications for the office of the pastor can be summarized into five categories:

1. Able to Teach

The ability to teach is the primary qualification that sets apart the work of a pastor from all others in the church. Paul writes that a man must be "able to teach" (1 Timothy 3:2). This qualification refers to more than just a desire to teach. It involves having the skill and ability to teach God's word faithfully, accurately, and effectively. Paul confirms this elsewhere when he writes that God has entrusted these men to guard the gospel— "the good deposit ... with the help of the Holy Spirit who lives in us" (2 Timothy 1:14).

This requirement of being able to teach should also be understood in light of what James writes about teachers. He warns that those who teach in the church "will be judged more strictly" (James 3:1). Those who have been gifted by God for this task should do so humbly, clearly, passionately, and faithfully. The call to teach involves preaching the word (2 Timothy 4:2) no matter what the cost, seizing every opportunity to make the gospel clear by presenting the treasure and value of Christ, calling people to repent and believe, and then trusting in the power of the Holy Spirit to transform hearts and minds. The ability to instruct God's people with his word is referred to as correcting, rebuking, and encouraging (2 Timothy 4:2), and it should define gospel ministry, both public and private. As the Baptist minister Roger Ellsworth has rightly observed, "Fail here and you would have failed in your central task."[13]

2. Have a Blameless Reputation

Paul's command that a pastor "is to be above reproach" (1 Timothy 3:2) is listed to emphasize that he should not just flee from evil but should seek to avoid even the appearance of evil. For example, it is hard to accuse a pastor of having an affair if everyone knows that a pastor will not be alone in a room with another woman (except his wife). The qualification to have a blameless reputation means that a pastor should seek to live in a way that avoids accusations. He should seek to live a consistent, godly life and cultivate a good reputation among all people. Not being in bondage to any substance but being self-controlled affirms this reputation, which seems to be why Paul also mentions that he should not be "given to drunkenness" (1 Timothy 3:3).

Having a blameless reputation also involves having a "good reputation with outsiders, so that he will not fall into disgrace and into the devil's trap" (1 Timothy 3:7). This does not mean backing down from the truth or trying to compromise with the world; it means living in a way that demonstrates God's love and compassion for the lost—that "they may see your good deeds and glorify God on the day he visits us" (1 Peter 2:12).

3. Faithfully Manage His Family

A third qualification for the call to be a pastor is to be "faithful to his wife" (1 Timothy 3:2). This phrase is commonly misunderstood to mean that a pastor must be married and cannot be single, but the phrase refers not to marital status but to faithfulness—that if a man is married, he is to be committed and faithful to his one wife. A pastor's leadership in the home is shown by the depth of his love for his wife, living sacrificially "just as Christ loved the church and gave himself up for her" (Ephesians 5:25). This command is given to all Christian husbands to love their wives in this way, but as a pastor he is called to model this for his people.

This qualification, when taken with Paul's additional instructions to Timothy, also indicates that a woman is not to assume authority over a man (1 Timothy 2:12). Just as men are to lead their families, God's design is for the men to lead the church.

This principle also applies to children living in a pastor's home. A pastor is to shepherd, teach, care, and manage his children faithfully (1 Timothy 3:4). This does not require that a pastor must have children or that his children must necessarily be converted. It means that a pastor's children must respect his authority as the God-appointed head and leader of the family. Why does this matter? Paul gives a profound reason: "If anyone does not know how to manage his own family, how can he take care of God's church?" (1 Timothy 3:5).

Along with managing his household, a pastor should be warm and welcoming toward outsiders and visitors to his home. He should be "hospitable" (1 Timothy 3:2). Most people only think of this as welcoming people into their home—and that is certainly an important element of hospitality—but hospitality more generally speaks of our disposition and attitude toward strangers. It's not difficult to be hospitable to people you know and love, but few of us are hospitable to strangers— people we don't know. Paul tells us that a pastor should model a willingness to care for others—even those he does not know. He also implies that a pastor should train his household to embrace this as a calling for the entire family.

4. Have a Godly Character

Most of the characteristics Paul lists can be lumped into the general category of godly character. Paul tells us that a pastor is to be "temperate, self-controlled, respectable" (1 Timothy 3:2), as well as "gentle, not quarrelsome" (1 Timothy 3:3). All of these qualities speak of the inward transformation of the gospel—of how Christ is reflected in a person as they are kind, compassionate, self-controlled with words and actions, honorable, humble, and full of discernment and wisdom. It is difficult to overstate the importance of this as a requirement for leadership and ministry. Basil Manly Jr. observed, "It need scarcely be said that *piety* is essential. No amount of talent, no extent of education, no apparent brilliancy of fervor, should ever be allowed to gain admission into the ministry for one whose piety there is a reason to doubt, or who has not a more than ordinary active and consistent holiness. A Christless minister is as horribly out of place as a ghastly skeleton in the pulpit, bearing a torch in his hand."[14]

Ministers should not just possess these godly characteristics; they should also evidence a pattern of growth in these qualities. The nineteenth-century Scottish minister David Dickson writes, "Though the work of eldership is in itself very honorable and very interesting, yet it will be dull, formal, and worthless, unless there be a real and growing love to Jesus in our hearts. That is the only oil that will make the lamp burn, and keep it burning."[15]

It is no accident that most of Paul's qualifications for pastoral ministry fall into the category of godly character. Those who desire the work of pastoral ministry should labor diligently to grow in these qualities, knowing it is the grace of God and the transforming power of the gospel that empower their growth.

5. Possess a Spiritual Maturity

Many of these qualities also point to the requirement of spiritual maturity, but I think there are two qualities in particular that indicate this. First, Paul tells us that a pastor is to be "not a lover of money" (1 Timothy 3:3). A pastor's primary responsibility is to preach and teach the word of God and sacrificially care for his people — not to seek financial gain for himself. Assessing whether a person is free of the love of money is not about how much money a pastor has or what he will get paid; it is about what the pastor does with the money he has. Having a love for money speaks to a desire to have more and more of it. A pastor should be compensated for the work he does, but a man should not enter the ministry out of a desire for personal material gain.

Secondly, as the spiritual leaders and doctrinal gatekeepers of the church, pastors "must not be a recent convert" (1 Timothy 3:6). This means a spiritually immature person should not enter this work, which makes sense for obvious reasons. In the text, though, Paul gives a specific one — lest "he may become conceited and fall under the same judgment as the devil." An immature believer could easily get caught up in the power of the position instead of seeing the office as a sacrifice and service to God and his people. Pursuing pastoral ministry also places a man on the front lines of spiritual attack from the enemy, which seems to be one of the several reasons the New Testament calls for a plurality of godly, spiritually mature pastors/elders in a local church. When multiple pastors and elders lead, it allows for greater accountability, richer fellowship, and deeper ways in which the church can benefit from their accumulated wisdom (Acts 20:28; Titus 1:5; 1 Peter 5:1).

A Christian Man Who Is Intimately Involved with the Local Church

No one would want to have a physician who just finished medical school but has no practical understanding of how a hospital works or no experience in treating sick people. Likewise, no one wants a pastor who is not involved in the very work he feels called to do — the ministry of the local church. A local church cannot rightly affirm someone who has not demonstrated the "desire and character" required for this office through actual involvement in ministry in the church. For a local church to extend an external call to someone, they must first see evidence confirming his calling in the ministry he does in the context of the church.

A Christian man's internal calling will be demonstrated through his love and commitment to his local church. Sadly, that is not the norm today. It is all too common for a young man to spend several years in seminary, cut off from any local church involvement. When he graduates, he wrongly assumes that a love for the church will magically accompany the salary he accepts from his first pastorate. But a love for the church is developed over time through a consistent commitment to serving others in the church. A man who is called to ministry by God realizes that the church is the means through which God is building his kingdom and accomplishing his purposes in the world.

A Christian man's internal calling will also be revealed to the members of a local congregation as he exercises his spiritual gifts. Paul gives us several lists of spiritual gifts in Scripture, and there are many gifts that a man called to the pastorate should possess and use. These include gifts of preaching and teaching publicly and privately, showing kindly care for the widows, being hospitable in his home, and sharing the gospel with unbelievers. As these gifts are exercised, they will bear fruit and impact the lives of people in the local church in clearly observable ways. There will be an evident aptness to teach by sowing fruitful seeds of the word into people's hearts. Some will note the kindness and gentleness he shows to an elderly woman who is in the hospital. A man may choose to give his money away to help a family in need in the church, or he may invite a lonely unmarried person to share a meal with his family after a church service. As this man's actions and words impact others in the church through deliberate and intimate involvement, it will be evident that God is equipping him. At some point, the local church's role is to affirm what is evident and confirm the internal calling that a brother may be sensing in an external call.

The words of Scripture and voices from church history provide helpful encouragement and guidance for a Christian man seeking to identify an internal calling from God. Yet the qualities and characteristics we have looked at are primarily of use to leaders in the local church as they seek to evaluate candidates for ministry, looking at their record of service and fruitfulness in ministry. A Christian man who zealously desires the work of ministry, is able to teach, cares faithfully for his family, and exudes a godly, blameless, and spiritually mature character is someone who can receive an external call.

But what about the church that issues the call? What kind of local church gives this external call to those who desire to receive it? What are the marks of a church that identify it as faithful to the ministry of the gospel? It is to this topic that we turn in the next chapter.

CHAPTER 4

EXPECTATION
Who Gives the Call?

Every man who believes alone, that he is called of God to the ministry, has reason to apprehend that he is under delusion.

John L. Dagg, *Manual of Theology: A Treatise on Church Order*

MOST OF US AREN'T GOOD at evaluating ourselves. We tend to either think too highly of ourselves, or we beat ourselves up unnecessarily. We see this most clearly when we ask a preacher to evaluate his own sermons. A preacher who thinks he has delivered a "home run" sermon will often be humbled to discover mediocre responses from the listeners. On the other hand, a preacher who is initially discouraged after a self-perceived "lemon" message may quickly learn that God has used it to bear great spiritual fruit. Time after time, we see that in God's grace and power he uses weak human vessels to accomplish his purposes. This tendency reveals our need to have other Christians who can speak into our life and aid us in self-evaluation.

This is especially true when a man is considering a call to full-time gospel ministry. The nineteenth-century Baptist minister and educator John L. Dagg speaks powerfully about this need as he writes about the external call, "Every man who believes alone, that he is called of God to the ministry, has reason to apprehend that he is under delusion. If he finds that those who give proof that they honor God and love the souls of men, do not discover his ministerial qualifications, he has reason to suspect that they do not exist."[16]

Because we are unable to accurately evaluate ourselves, God gives us brothers and sisters in our local church who can fill this role.

To this point, I have said it is the responsibility of the local church to test, train, affirm, and send out those who pursue gospel ministry. But if we have never seen this process at work in our church, we may wonder, "What kind of church does this?" While the responsibility for the external call is not one of the essential marks of a true church of Jesus Christ,[17] it is a mark of a faithful church, one that is seeking to honor Christ and his word. Samuel Miller, who taught at Princeton Theological Seminary in the nineteenth century, observed, "No church, therefore, which neglects the proper education of her ministers, can be considered as faithful, either to her own most vital interests, or to the honour of her divine Head and Lord."[18]

The Marks of a Faithful Church

We'll begin by looking at the marks of a faithful and healthy church. Keep in mind that there is no such thing as a perfect church, but there are churches that strive to function, as best they can, in the way God has revealed in the Bible. I suggest four areas of faithfulness are essential if a church wishes to grow and be effective in giving an external call: the centrality of Scripture, faithful shepherding, regenerate church membership, and the practice of church discipline.

The Centrality of Scripture

A faithful church is one whose central focus and practice is determined by the words of Scripture. We live in a time when entertainment and pragmatism drive much of the practice of ministry in the evangelical church. Only a local church whose foundation for their faith and practice is God's word will be truly equipped to test, train, affirm, and send. Obedience to Christ's commands presupposes a knowledge of these commands.

The first way in which the centrality of Scripture is seen is in how leaders preach and teach God's word. Expositional preaching is the most effective way to make God's word central in a sermon or service. In his book *Nine Marks of a Healthy Church*, Mark Dever writes, "Expositional preaching is that preaching which takes for the point of a sermon the point of a particular passage of Scripture."[19] This is best accomplished through regular, systematic preaching on individual books of the Bible. This doesn't mean other approaches to preaching are bad or wrong, nor does it mean they can't be effective or fruitful. Still, a commitment to some level of expositional, systematic preaching through the books of the Bible is a clear indicator that a local church is seeking to be centered on God's word. This type of preaching provides a steady diet of spiritual nourishment for a hungry congregation.

In addition to expositional preaching, biblical theology should be a regular part of the instruction of a church. Biblical theology involves teaching the broad story line of the Bible, with God's redemptive purposes in Christ always in view. Ultimately, this helps us to read, study, and understand the Bible more clearly. Without the proper instruction of God's word in the church, not only will those called into ministry be confused, but spiritual life will be lacking in the church as well.

A commitment to the centrality of the word can also be seen in the polity or structure of the church. Though polity structures can vary from church to church, Scripture still gives us a template that is clear. The New Testament speaks of pastors/elders (1 Timothy 3:1 – 7) who are entrusted to preach and teach God's word and shepherd God's people (1 Peter 5:1 – 4). Deacons (1 Timothy 3:8 – 13) serve in the particular and practical ministries of the church. The congregation also plays a role, especially in the practice of church discipline (Matthew 18:15 – 17; 1 Corinthians 5:1 – 11). Those who serve in roles of leadership should conform to biblical qualifications. A clear biblical structure in a church provides the proper authority and oversight for those pursuing a call into the ministry, modeling the calling they wish to pursue.

A third area that reveals a commitment to the centrality of Scripture revolves around the types of ministry a local church chooses to engage in — or, to put it more clearly, why a church engages in certain ministries and not others. A church may serve by having some form of discipleship training, being intentional about evangelism, carrying out a mercy ministry, visiting the sick, or caring for widows, but the real question to ask is why. Why does the church do these things? The answer will reveal how dependent the church is on God's word. Some churches will emphasize numerical growth or love of neighbor as the basis for their ministry. But numbers and approval of people are not the motives for our ministry. Churches should be motivated to ministry for the glory of God and out of obedience to the commands of Scripture. If ministries exist in our church because Scripture prescribes them, this shows that the faith and practice of the church are centered on Scripture. A church like this is thereby equipped to give an external call to someone.

Faithful Shepherding of God's People

A local church should have pastors who shepherd and care for God's people. As we saw in chapter 1, a shepherd loves, guides, protects, and closely involves himself with his sheep. This is what Peter means when he exhorts the elders to "be shepherds of God's flock that is under your care" (1 Peter 5:2). Faithfully shepherding the flock implies deliberate involvement in the lives of the people, especially those who sense an internal call into the ministry. Being relationally involved is crucial to identifying if someone has the desire, the gifts, and the character needed to become a shepherd. Sometimes it may be necessary for a pastor to challenge a brother to consider pursuing the ministry, someone who had not previously considered it.

Though this may be obvious, it bears pointing out that pastors who faithfully shepherd their people model faithful shepherding to those who desire the same work. Peter exhorts elders to shepherd by "being examples to the flock" (1 Peter 5:3). A medical student learns best from shadowing a doctor as they interact with their patients. A law student learns most effectively from watching lawyers practice law. Likewise, a young man desiring to be a shepherd will be best equipped for the task by watching, learning, and imitating their pastor's care of them and others in the church.

Finally, a faithful shepherd instructs his flock in their responsibility to test, train, affirm, and send those seeking an external call. If the leaders never talk about this responsibility, the church won't know how to give the external call. A faithful, healthy church is one in which those who hold the office of pastor talk about the need to identify, train, and send out faithful leaders and pastors.

Regenerate Church Membership

A local church that gives an external call should have a regenerate church membership. By "regenerate" I mean that those covenant members of a local congregation who profess to follow Christ live lives that testify to the reality of their transformed hearts. This distinction may seem unnecessary to some, as most evangelicals believe that entrance into the church comes through a profession of faith in Christ. Yet despite this, we still hear reports from the Southern Baptist Convention that less than half of its recorded members attend a local church weekly. Other churches do not value membership and a profession of faith may not be required, so a distinction is needed. If the membership of a local church is not regenerate, it will negatively affect the process of identifying, affirming, and calling people to pastoral ministry.

Just as only a born-again believer in Christ can know and identify the fruit of salvation in another believer, so only a believer in Christ can identify and affirm a person who is called to shepherd other believers in the church. It does not matter that a person's father helped build the church or that he gave large amounts of money to the church. If his heart and mind have not been transformed by the gospel, he will be blind to the importance of the biblical qualifications for ministry and won't be able to recognize or identify those called by God to serve his church.

In addition, it will be difficult for unregenerate members to be involved in the process of testing, training, affirming, and sending. All of this requires a measure of godly discernment, as well as selflessness and a willingness to see others leave their fellowship for the advancement of other churches. Members should love the church and have a broad desire to see local churches healthy and the kingdom of God advance. A heart that is hardened to Christ and to the gospel cannot do this and will likely work against the church.

This is especially evident in congregational churches. A pastor-led congregational church will expect that it is the members who ultimately confirm other members into the church, make important decisions in the church, and affirm those seeking an external call. That call cannot be accurately given if a local church fails to take membership seriously.

The Practice of Church Discipline
A local church that extends an external call should also practice church discipline. Church discipline is the process that a local church initiates toward a member who is discovered to be sinning and shows no signs of genuine repentance of that sin. The recovery of church discipline is desperately needed in the twenty-first-century church. John Dagg, writing on this need,

declares that "when discipline leaves a church, Christ goes with it."[20] What makes church discipline so necessary?

The first reason is that discipline is biblical. It is a sign of love that a church extends to its members. The Bible clearly teaches that God disciplines those he loves and calls his own (Hebrews 12:4–8). And God tells us we should judge ourselves (2 Corinthians 13:5; 2 Peter 1:5–10). We are instructed to examine one another in the church and, if necessary, discipline those who have sinned (Matthew 18:15–17; 1 Corinthians 5:1–11; Galatians 6:1; 2 Thessalonians 3:6–15). God's design is for church discipline to be a regular, normal part of the life of a healthy church.

The second reason, as I've already hinted, is that discipline is actually for the benefit of the members of the church. God did not intend for us to pursue the Christian life in isolation. God has always intended for us to be in community with others—"to correct, rebuke and encourage—with great patience and careful instruction" (2 Timothy 4:2). Some wrongly conclude that church discipline is unloving when in actuality it is one of the most loving things we can do for a brother or sister in the church who is blinded to the reality and effects of sin in his or her life. Scripture repeatedly affirms that church discipline is done for the benefit of the local church as a whole. This discipline should be done gently, with restoration in mind (Galatians 6:1) and for the sake of a person's eternal soul (1 Corinthians 5:1–11). Discipline should also be practiced to help other members see that sin has serious consequences, as a deterrent (1 Timothy 5:20). God designed church discipline to be a loving, helpful, and necessary tool to assist one another in faithfully following our Savior.

Expectation

The third reason for practicing church discipline follows from the previous two reasons. Church discipline is a necessary part of testing, training, affirming, and sending out those who are called into gospel ministry. Where there is a willingness to discipline those in sin out of love for them, it will create a culture in which hard, potentially painful things can be shared with a brother or sister for that person's benefit. Churches that want to faithfully test and train candidates for ministry must be able to speak the truth in love. For example, a church may decide that an individual is not qualified or ready. Instead of affirming his call, they should be ready to lovingly suggest he not pursue the call to pastoral ministry. Likewise, a church may have times when they need to affirm and send a brother, even if the road will involve a great sacrifice or be life threatening. A church may need to send a family into a mission field where persecution is likely. They may need to affirm a brother in his decision to take a $100,000 pay cut from his marketing job to pastor a small church in the country. These decisions cannot be taken lightly. The truth must be spoken, even if it is not comfortable.

God can and will use any church that strives to be faithful to the gospel of Jesus Christ. And when a local church also pursues faithfulness and health in these four areas, it will be a healthier church—one that is better equipped to give an external call to those who seek it.

Up to this point, we have looked at the internal and external call, as well as who gives the call and who receives the call. But how does all of this work in practice? What is the process of recognizing, training, and affirming the call? In the next chapter, we'll turn to some of these practical considerations.

CHAPTER 5

APPLICATION
How to Proceed in the Call?

> In regard to these qualifications, the
> churches are usually better judges than the
> individual himself, and must exercise their
> judgment with prudence and fidelity, under
> a solemn sense of their accountability, and
> "lay not careless hands on heads that can-
> not teach and will not learn."
>
> Basil Manly Jr.,
> "Testing a Call to the Ministry"

WE SHOULD NEVER ASSUME that just because someone has
head knowledge and can talk as if they know how something
is done, they actually know how to do it. A person may get
quite excited about skydiving because they just read a book
about it, but that individual is no more prepared to actually
skydive than a person is ready to preach because they heard a
good sermon. Don't assume that after reading the first four
chapters of this book, you know what is involved in testing,
training, affirming, and sending those who are called into
ministry. Applying what you have learned to your own local
church context is essential. Wisdom is learned through trial
and error, as we put all of this into practice.

Application

Earlier, we looked at a key passage in Acts 13 — the calling of Saul and Barnabas. But this is simply a snapshot of a moment in a particular church and a particular culture. It is helpful, but we need to remember that the Bible does not give us a detailed, line-by-line procedure for testing and training those who feel called to be pastors. With this in mind, I preface this chapter by saying that most of these suggestions come from the efforts I have made in our own local church, applications that we have found helpful and beneficial.

Testing

Paul tells us in his letter to the Ephesian church that God gives some men to the church who are apostles, prophets, evangelists, and pastors and teachers for the equipping and building up of the church (Ephesians 4:11 – 12). How do you find these men in your own local church context? The best way we have found is to test those who sense an internal calling to this work. Testing involves exposing an individual to a variety of different, real-life circumstances to observe how they handle them. So the best way to test men for the office of pastor is to evaluate them in situations in which they do the work of a pastor, taking into consideration the qualifications mapped out in Scripture (1 Timothy 3:1 – 7; Titus 1:5 – 9). Over time, we can begin to determine whether a young man who desires this work is truly called, especially as his gifts to preach and teach are tested. This is a testing that should be done visibly before the congregation.

For example, in our church we have twelve different men preach on a different psalm on Sunday evenings every summer.

These are men who want to test their gifts to preach. This is not only an opportunity for them to serve our church; it is also a way for us to consider their giftedness as a church body. We encourage church members to approach each individual after the service to give specific comments of encouragement and critique in a loving, helpful way. In addition, a mandatory service review is held after the Sunday evening service, in which the pastors and a few other men who are testing their gifts speak kindly, yet truthfully into this brother's life, giving feedback about the sermon.* Encouragement is given, corrections are made, and suggestions are helpfully submitted so he can improve for the next opportunity.

These brothers are also tested when they visit church members' homes. They are going out to offer care for an individual member, and at the same time a pastor or elder observes them or gathers feedback from others to determine how they are serving. We will pay attention to how self-controlled, hospitable, gentle, peaceful, above reproach, and respectable a person is—all qualities Paul highlights (1 Timothy 3:1–7; Titus 1:5–9). As a brother visits different members, the pastors will either go with him or informally check to see how the visit went and what fruit seemed to come from it. When a brother who desires the work of a shepherd is confronted with the care of a dying saint in the hospital who needs a word of comfort, the ground of testing is significantly plowed.

In the kind providence of God, every portion of an individual's testing works for the good of the local church as a whole. When a brother preaches, he is feeding God's people through

---

* See appendix 2.

his labor in the word. When a brother disciples another brother in the congregation, he is helping him mature and grow in his faith in Christ. When a brother visits a church member confined to home or a member in the hospital, they are caring for the soul of that church member and ultimately serving the pastors and church as a whole in their efforts. As they serve the church in the midst of this testing, they are beginning to learn the daily labors of ministry — things that can't be learned from reading books or taking classes. This is the start of hands-on training for the ministry.

Training

When testing is done more frequently and intentionally, it becomes training. By this time, the pastors of the church have identified to some degree the gifts in an individual (according to 1 Timothy 3:1 – 7) that need to be deliberately developed. At this point, a brother begins to play a more active role in the church's leadership — regularly teaching classes, leading services, or preaching for an entire month on Sunday evenings. This person is now someone the pastors trust to send on a hospital visit on his own or to gain more exposure to the decisions and directions of the church. They may be involved in evaluating the sermons and the services every week. In all these efforts, they are being trained for ministry, while the members of the church continue to be served, encouraged, and cared for through their efforts.

At a recent commissioning service for missionaries of our congregation, I exhorted a family that had been through this stage of the process.

You, _____ [husband and wife], have been in many of our homes and us in yours. We have had the joy of fellowship with you. You have served our church in so many ways. You, _____ [wife], have cared for our children as you have faithfully cared for your own. You modeled a Christlike attitude through a very difficult family schedule. You, _____ [husband], have faithfully preached and taught God's word to us. You have helped several people spiritually grow through your discipleship efforts. You, _____ [husband], have helped lead our public gatherings and have used your pastoral experience to help the pastors think through some difficult issues. However, as we fellowshipped together and served with you both, something else was happening—you were being tested and trained before our eyes for the work to which you felt called. By God's grace, he has allowed our church the joy of Christian fellowship with you through that time to put us in a place to affirm you.

The specific details of the training will vary depending on the gifts of the individual and the ministry to which they are called. But the key is that the training is centered within the local church, is led by the pastors, and comes to expression in ministry to the members of the local church. Ultimately, this is what allows a local church to be in a position where it can affirm a man's gifts and calling.

Affirming

After the pastors and leaders have had adequate time to test and train a brother pursuing the ministry, the time comes when they must decide to affirm them or not affirm them.

Application

After prayer and thoughtful discussion, if the pastors feel a brother does possess an internal call, we recommend him to the congregation for a more formal time of evaluation. Because much of his testing and training has been visibly done with and in the presence of the people of the church, they should be informed enough to make their own decision. Often, we will have helpful and fruitful discussions in our members' meetings, and if there are no concerns raised, the church comes back after a month of praying to vote to affirm the call.

This affirmation can happen in several different ways. It may be an affirmation for a brother to serve as an assistant pastor in our church. It may be an affirmation for him to leave for another local church to pursue a ministry position. It may be a vote to affirm a couple who desires to enter the mission field. It may be to affirm someone whom the church is sending to plant a church elsewhere in the city. Regardless of specific details of the affirmation, the decision to ordain a brother as a pastor or missionary should involve a public affirmation, which serves as a sign that they have the full support of our local church.

Here is an excerpt of a public statement I once made to our church about a family that was pursuing missionary service. I hope it reveals clearly the kind of scrutiny we use when evaluating those who sense an internal calling.

I have had one-on-one meetings with this couple to discuss their marriage, family, educational challenges, and struggles with sin. The pastors have discussed their situation on numerous occasions. We have had several public discussions about this family at our members' meetings. Yet, they still sit here desiring our affirmation, because in all those discussions, we as a church have felt convinced, though the road they face will be hard, that this is the work the Lord has for them.

Statements such as these are designed to remind the congregation that we've carried out a testing and training process to get to that point. It also indicates that the time has now come to affirm the call. I've made similar statements to the congregation when someone is pursuing pastoral ministry in a local church.

I have had one-on-one meetings with _____ and his wife about their marriage. We have watched him shepherd his wife and children faithfully, thereby demonstrating faithful management of his household. He has demonstrated that he is gifted to teach and preach through his faithful labor of the word among us. He has been in many of your homes, where he has displayed his love for you and your souls. He has been to visit many of you in the hospital, where he has brought the comfort of the gospel in your time of need. He has conducted himself in our church with self-control, gentleness, kindness, patience, and a moral character that is above reproach. Though the struggles of pastoral ministry will challenge every area we have tested and trained him in, we are confident of the Lord's hand on him for this work.

Regardless of the structure of your polity, every local congregation should eventually come to a point of affirmation. Once an individual has been tested, trained, and affirmed by the leaders and congregation, we are ready to do what God has called us to do—send them out!

Application

Sending

Sending someone out from a local church can be a complicated and involved process. They may be pursuing a pastorate or working in the mission field, or they may simply be taking a step toward getting a theological education. In each case, we as a church commit several things as we send them out. We are committing to pray regularly for them, to give wisdom and pastoral oversight regarding where they should go, and to be in regular contact with them while they are serving elsewhere. A church may also need to make a financial commitment, especially if the individual or family goes to a mission field where they won't be funded by a particular person or organization. When we have individuals pursuing theological education, we work to make sure there is oversight and that he will be involved in a local church as he attends school. Sending is never the end of the process. It is the start of a new commitment by a local church to give those who have been tested, trained, affirmed, and sent out our blessing and support.

The sending process is most tangibly seen when we hold a special service to recognize the external call. These services are often referred to as ordination or commissioning services. An individual has already been affirmed, so this ceremony acts as a more formal way of acknowledging that they have gifts and are called to the work of ministry. The service can contain vows repeated by those being sent and by the congregation that is sending them.[21] A sermon should be preached that points to the biblical qualifications required, the work and ministry they are called to do, or the responsibility of the local church in affirming them. The content of the service can vary, offering instruction, encouragement, and challenge to both the individual and the congregation.

The most important part of the service is when pastors and church leaders lay their hands on the individual and pray for them and the ministry to which they are being called. This follows the model in the Antioch church (Acts 13:3). The act of laying on hands and praying is not a mystical transfer that somehow changes the individual. It simply marks in a visible way the conclusion of a process of testing, training, and affirmation by the pastors and members of the congregation. It also represents in a visible way that the authority Christ has given to his church is being extended to this individual. Basil Manly Jr., one of the founding fathers of The Southern Baptist Theological Seminary, emphasized the responsibility the local church has in identifying those who qualify as ministers of the gospel and how the laying on of hands symbolizes that authority: "In regard to these qualifications, the churches are usually better judges than the individual himself, and must exercise their judgment with prudence and fidelity, under a solemn sense of their accountability, and 'lay not careless hands on heads that cannot teach and will not learn.'"[22]

Here is one way I have explained the laying on of hands to our congregation during a service of commission: "In a few moments, we will do what the church in Antioch did (Acts 13:3). We will lay hands on each of you and pray, sealing our affirmation of you to pursue these opportunities of ministry by God's grace."

While the laying on of hands is not a supernatural event in which the individuals prayed for are now somehow more ready and prepared for the task than before, it is significant. As pastors and leaders lay their hands on the individual, they should pray for fruitfulness in ministering the gospel. They should pray for faithfulness in the proclamation of God's word. They should pray that the individual and his family will be protected from the evil one. They should pray for the development of a growing zeal and passion for the work to which he has been called. They should pray for Christ's presence by his Spirit to be with them. They should pray for purity, for a hatred of sin, as well as for a man to be faithful in loving his wife as Christ loved the church and to responsibly shepherd his children. They should pray that God's kingdom will continue to advance.

All of this is significant because God will answer these prayers. He will empower those who ask for his help. Just like the Antioch church, we, by faith, believe that as we send them out, the Spirit also sends them out (Acts 13:3–4).

Three Key Roles

Finally, let me add some final words to you, the one reading this book. I don't know who you are, but I'm going to assume you fit into one of three key roles in the calling process—a pastor, someone sensing a call to the ministry, or a regular faithful church member.

1. A Pastor

It takes a pastor to recognize a potential pastor. As you look for those who might have the gift to serve in pastoral ministry, try to look past the apparent immaturity so you can discern who might have a special gift from God to teach his word and care for his people. Even if you don't have a formal process for identifying and testing a person, you can start by taking them to the hospital with you. Let them tag along when you visit shut-ins. When you think they're ready, let them teach a Sunday school class one week or lead a small group Bible study, so you can observe them in that role. Begin teaching your congregation about their responsibility to identify and train candidates for ministry. The process begins with you. It won't be a priority in your already busy life of ministry if you don't see the need for it.

2. Those Who Sense a Call

If you are someone who desires to do the work of a pastor or missionary, let me first encourage you—this is, as Paul said, "a noble task" (1 Timothy 3:1)! My hope, as you've read this book, is that you do not just rely on your internal call or your own abilities to develop your gifts, but that you place yourself under the authority of a local church and trust that God will work through the pastors and believers in that congregation to affirm your internal call with an external call. Take every opportunity to serve and care for the souls of the people in your church. Take every opportunity you are given to teach or preach. Humbly serve the church in the smallest of ways, trusting that God is preparing you for every future opportunity to minister the gospel to someone. Trust that God is not only at work in you as you pursue this calling, but that he is at work in your local church to affirm that which you feel called to do.

3. A Faithful Church Member

Thank you for taking the time to read this book. You may not feel called to pastoral ministry, but you clearly care about the health of your church and want to see godly leaders trained and called into ministry. Your responsibility is to continue to do what a faithful church member does—invest and pour your life into the people of the church so that when the time comes to affirm someone for the ministry, you are well informed. When a young, inexperienced brother is given an opportunity to teach Sunday school or preach on a Sunday evening, take the time to go and listen attentively. They may not be the best preacher you've ever heard and may need help to grow, but you can always encourage them by sharing what you thought they did well and lovingly correct them as to how they can do better. Put your personal preferences aside and try to avoid comparisons. Embrace the opportunity to be part of helping someone grow and learn through this experience. If a young man asks to visit you, love and encourage him as he makes the effort to learn how to minister to you. God has a specific role for every member in the process of testing, training, affirming, and sending those called into the ministry. Do you see your need to be faithful and to play your role?

The primary reason churches give for deciding not to train leaders and affirm their calling is an inability to know how to move forward practically. My hope is that you'll realize the specific details aren't as important as the willingness to be the church that God has designed you to be. May the outworking of the external call in this chapter spark ways in which this process can become a reality for you, your church, and those in your church who await your commitment to put forth the work to test, train, affirm, and send them.

CHAPTER 6

FAITHFULNESS

What Is at Stake with This Call?

> It is a fearful calamity to a man to miss his calling, and to the church upon whom he imposes himself, his mistake involves an affliction of the most grievous kind.
>
> Charles H. Spurgeon,
> *Lectures to My Students*

THE FINEST BIOGRAPHY of the eighteenth-century evangelist George Whitefield is arguably Arnold Dallimore's two-volume work. In it, Dallimore captures the life and times of this great historical figure and shows how Whitefield's love for Christ and the souls of men compelled him to preach bold, powerful, and oftentimes controversial sermons. It produced a passion to raise funds to serve children cared for by his orphanage and moved him to speak against many social injustices as he traveled throughout America and Great Britain.

Another portion of Whitefield's mission — one largely overlooked but developed brilliantly by Dallimore, is Whitefield's zeal to speak against the unconverted and unfaithful who were filling pulpits all across New England in that era. In a journal entry after Whitefield had attended a service in New

York, he explains why he chose to take on such a controversial issue: "Went to the English church, both morning and evening. Felt my heart almost bleed within me, to consider what blind guides were sent forth into her. If I have any regard for the honor of Christ, and good of souls, I must lift up my voice like a trumpet, and shew how sadly our Church ministers are fallen from the doctrines of the Reformation."[23]

As Whitefield shook pulpits across New England with the powerful preaching of the gospel, he also shook up many of these wolves in sheep's clothing, men who regularly preached each Sunday morning. Unsurprisingly, Whitefield's efforts were met with great hostility and opposition. As Dallimore accurately observes, "In the apathy of the times, the principle 'A converted minister is best, but an unconverted one cannot fail to do some good' had become almost everywhere accepted."[24]

For this reason, Whitefield attacked this destructive pattern in the church with the same zeal with which he attacked lost souls in the fields of open-air preaching. He knew what was at stake if certain men who had not been called to do so filled pulpits and were charged to shepherd God's people.

In considering the responsibility of the local church to issue the external call for ministry, we must understand exactly what is at stake if the local church fails in her task. Before we do so, however, let's talk about what's not at stake. We need to firmly hold to Jesus' promise that he will build his church, and the gates of Hades will not overcome it (Matthew 16:18). We need to remember that God's work of redemption is a finished work in the sufficient sacrifice of Jesus Christ (Hebrews 1:3; 10:14).

We know that God has chosen a people before the foundation of the world (Ephesians 1:4) from every tribe and language and people and nation — those who have been purchased by the blood of the Lamb and who will be brought into the kingdom of God as the gospel is preached among all the nations (Revelation 5:9 – 10). These truths are biblical certainties — things that are contingent not on our faithfulness to the external call but on the sovereign purposes of our faithful God.

Yet we should also recognize that God accomplishes these purposes by working in and through his people. Because this is true, much is at stake in our own lives as individuals and in the well-being of local churches. Ultimately, the name of Christ is not lifted up and his glory manifested as clearly if local churches refuse to be faithful to the external call.

Individual Christians

I love football, especially professional football. I love to watch games, and when I watch them, a desire to get out there and play wells up within me. If I allowed myself to dwell too much on the euphoria of that feeling, I could probably convince myself to get to a game or a practice and try out for a team. But what do you think would happen to me? What if I actually had a chance to play in a professional football game? On the very first play I would be crushed! It doesn't matter how much I think I am ready to play — just one head-on collision with a three-hundred-pound lineman will force me back to reality. The harm and injury I face from taking a hit like that can be avoided if someone lovingly tells me what is obvious to everyone: "You're too old and too small, and you do not possess the gifts to survive playing in a professional football game."

There are those who are doing the work of shepherding God's people, but they are not gifted or called to do so. By continuing in this role, they risk much harm to the sheep and great pain and disappointment for themselves as well. We once had a young man in our church who wanted to be a pastor and even demonstrated some gifts that led him in that direction. Unfortunately, certain aspects of his life concerned us as his pastors. We discouraged him from pursuing the ministry — primarily because of his difficult and fragile marriage.

At one point, he called a meeting to let us know he was interested in applying for an associate pastor position and wanted to know if we would affirm him for the position. As painful as it was for us, we decided that in good conscience we could not recommend him to the congregation at that time because of his growing marriage difficulties. He rejected our counsel, was accepted for the ministry position, and left our church with resentment. Sadly, his marriage problems escalated with the pressures of pastoral ministry, and eventually his wife took their children and left him. Though our relationship has since been mended, his relationship with his wife has not been restored. This is just one example of why the local church must take this responsibility seriously, realizing what is at stake. Pastors and leaders must caution and discourage any individual who is unable to evaluate himself accurately.

The Health of the Church

George Whitefield pronounces a death sentence on churches that contain unfaithful shepherds when he writes, "The reason why congregations have been so dead is, because they have had dead men preaching to them."[25] There are churches that have dead men (spiritually) preaching to them, prideful men guiding them, and greedy men abusing them. There are countless stories of unfaithful shepherds who harm the sheep. Stories abound of pastors abusing their position to embezzle money or sexually pursue a vulnerable married woman in the congregation. Scandals like these not only bring great harm to the individuals involved; they mar the reputation of the church of Christ.

I once served on the staff of a large church alongside a pastor who had some questionable financial practices. Whenever someone confronted the pastor about this, they were silenced or fired. Most tried to ignore the rumors and just focused on their own area of ministry. Two years after I left that church, the pastor was investigated, and it was discovered that he had traded hundreds of thousands of dollars of the church's money in the stock market — losing it all. To make matters worse, the new pastor who replaced him was later caught in an adulterous affair and had to leave the ministry. These two men caused incalculable harm to this local church.

Disqualifying sins can creep into the lives of even the most faithful of pastors. Those in gospel ministry are on the front lines and regularly experience the attacks of the enemy. They must learn to be on guard at all times and should surround themselves with faithful men who can hold them accountable. There is great risk in welcoming an unfaithful shepherd into leadership, giving them authority, power, influence, and position. This is why it is essential that churches only affirm and send those who truly have been called.

Theological Education

Seminaries and Bible colleges are a wonderful resource for training those called by God. These institutions faithfully educate future pastors and missionaries. Yet seminaries cannot replace the unique role of the local church. As we saw in chapter 2, institutions of theological education have wrongfully been given this responsibility, and when they assume this role, they are distracted from their primary purpose.

I once met with the supervisor of an applied ministry program of a seminary and asked him why so few hours were dedicated to the practical side of ministry. My question presumed it was the seminary's responsibility to do this training. The supervisor told me that increasing the requirements for applied ministry would mean decreasing the requirements in other areas, adding more work to an already full schedule for students. But the responsibility for this applied training doesn't lie with the seminary—it lies with the local church. The answer is not to increase course loads and add more classes. Institutions of theological education should focus on what they do best—teaching the original languages, plumbing the depths of systematic theology, and covering the span of church history.

The local church should work alongside theological institutions to prepare gospel ministers. Without this kind of functioning "marriage," it puts a harmful burden on the school. When these two entities are able to work together, the result is fruitful training. We saw this in our own church when two young, single brothers attended our local seminary and at the same time remained members of our church, faithfully serving and submitting themselves to the pastors. During the week they were immersed in studying Greek and Hebrew. On Sundays they effectively taught Sunday school classes. During the week they were occupied with writing systematic theology and church history papers late at night, yet they found time to care for the widows and visit the sick.

Some churches do not have a local seminary or training institution in their area. In those cases, the scenario might involve a season at seminary followed by a season serving within a local church. Regardless of the specifics, a fruitful result is still achievable. It will always require that local churches accept their role and theological institutions release students to serve in local churches. The long-term health of the church, as well as the effectiveness of these theological institutions, is at stake.

The Glory of Christ

God's plan is that the corporate witness of the redeemed in the local church will display the glory of Jesus Christ to a lost and dying world. But this corporate witness will be distorted if shepherds who aren't called by God are placed in positions of influence and authority. When Christians follow a shepherd who is not truly called by God, it can lead them to believe false teaching and adopt ungodly lifestyles, and they will lose sight of their purpose as a church. This hinders the spread of the gospel to the nations, especially when missionaries who are not equipped for the task are sent to the field. Sadly, there are too many stories of missionaries who went to the field with little time spent in preparation. They were never tested, examined, or held accountable by their local church. As a result, they were negatively affected by the pagan cultures in which they were immersed. Often, missionaries in these circumstances become discouraged or become soft on the essentials of doctrine as they undergo the intense spiritual attacks of the enemy. Others become ineffective or muddy the clear waters of the gospel. The local church must faithfully test, train, affirm, and send pastors and missionaries, or else it will negatively impact the progress of the gospel, the corporate witness of the church, and the renown and glory of Jesus.

Though our primary motivation for being faithful in all of this is obedience to Scripture, I end this chapter on a note of warning. My hope is that these words will serve as a sober reminder of what is truly at stake if the local church fails to recover this essential responsibility for the external call.

CONCLUSION

> Is it not worth all our labours and sufferings
> ... to hear one spiritual child say, Lord, this
> is the minister by whom I believed: Another,
> this is he, by whom I was edified, estab-
> lished, and comforted. This is the man that
> resolved my doubts, quickened my dying
> affections, reduced my soul, when wander-
> ing from the truth!
>
> John Flavel, "The Character of a Complete
> Evangelical Pastor, Drawn by Christ"

THE ARGUMENT I HAVE LAID BEFORE YOU in this short book
is biblical, but it is also a reflection of the commitment and
convictions of our local church—Auburndale Baptist Church
in Louisville, Kentucky. As we have put these truths into practice, we have experienced the joys (and sorrows) that come with
the responsibility to give the external call. As this book comes
to an end, I want to share a story, an illustration of how all of
this works—albeit imperfectly—in a local church.

A young married man who had two children moved to Louisville to attend seminary. He and his wife came from a solid,
healthy, and faithful local church where he had been discipled,
taught well, and given opportunities to serve. As he began to
sense an internal call to pastoral ministry, he approached the

elders of his church and asked them what they thought of him leaving to attend seminary. They acknowledged he had certain gifts that could be used in pastoral ministry. They took some steps to begin observing more intentionally how he lived, how he used his gifts, and how effective he was as a teacher. After a period of time, he was affirmed by the leadership and the church and left with their full support to attend seminary and pursue a calling to pastoral ministry.

He and his family arrived in Louisville and decided to settle in at our church. Early on, this family demonstrated a deep commitment to the local church. Whether it was serving in the nursery, engaging in hospitality, discipling others, doing evangelism, taking his family to visit the sick and widows, or cutting down trees around the church, this brother demonstrated a love for Christ, a love for God's people, and a strong desire to do the work of a pastor. Because of this desire and the faithfulness he showed, we allowed him opportunities to preach and teach. Our pastors and the congregation were encouraged as we saw the fruitfulness of his service and his personal spiritual growth as a follower of Christ.

Yet, like all of us, maturing in Christ does not come without struggles and the attacks of the enemy. The stress of working a job, managing a full load of school, and juggling family and church life wore him down, and he struggled with discouragement. He sought out the pastors for care and encouragement, and he modeled the way a brother should seek spiritual care when dark times come. Eventually, he resumed his labor in our church with a seemingly greater zeal than before. By his grace, God used this dark time of struggle to mature this brother in special ways that caused him to have a greater love for the gospel, burden for the struggles of our people, and capacity to shepherd God's people in our church.

At this time, he was officially put forward and affirmed as a pastor of our congregation. During this time, his fruitfulness as a preacher and shepherd continued to grow. He was wise, insightful, and discerning in many difficult and challenging situations faced by the pastors. He led the congregation through a painful discipline process that resulted in the removal of a church member. We enjoyed sweet fellowship with him and his family, and it was undeniable that he had an internal calling to the work of a pastor.

After serving for a time in our congregation and completing his theological education, he was sent with the full support and affirmation of our church to serve as senior pastor of another church. We were sad to send him out, because of our loss, but we were also filled with joy at the gain of this church. To this day, he continues to serve faithfully in that church. As his sending church, we continue to pray for him regularly and support him in whatever way he needs, and we rejoice in the privilege of being part of what the Lord is doing through this brother's faithful gospel-centered ministry.

This past year, we sent another man from our local church who had also been through a season of testing and training, and we affirmed and sent him to go and serve alongside this man as his associate pastor. In God's kind providence, the former pastor was intimately involved in the discipling, mentoring, and instructing of this younger brother who now serves as his associate.

Conclusion

One of the great joys we have as pastors — one shared by our entire congregation — is to see our passion for faithful gospel-centered preaching, the tireless shepherding of God's people, and the building of Christ's kingdom outside our local church multiply through these brothers. Without a doubt, there are many struggles and sorrows that accompany this task. Yet we labor in this task because we desire that shepherds and the sheep cared for by them in the local church around the world experience what the great Puritan pastor John Flavel captured so powerfully:

> O brethren! Who would not study and pray, spend and be spent, in the service of such a bountiful Master! Is it not worth all our labours and sufferings, to come with all those souls we instrumentally begat to Christ: and all that we edified, established, confirmed, and comforted in the way to heaven; and say, *Lord, here am I, and the children thou hast given me?* To hear one spiritual child say, Lord this is the minister by whom I believed: Another, this is he, by whom I was edified, established, and comforted. This is the man that resolved my doubts, quickened my dying affections, reduced my soul, when wandering from the truth![26]

For this reason, let me encourage you to take up the responsibility to test, train, affirm, and send those into gospel ministry that our bountiful Master has entrusted to us. Let us do this to be faithful, but also in great anticipation of that glorious day when our Chief Shepherd appears, and we are able to celebrate all those who receive that unfading crown of glory — the crown that is promised to all who are called, faithful, and steadfast shepherds of the Lord Jesus Christ (1 Peter 5:4).

ACKNOWLEDGMENTS

A SPECIAL THANKS TO—

Matt Crawford, Jason Adkins, Adam Embry, and Greg Van Court for your friendship, gospel partnership, and willingness to exercise your gifts to improve immensely the clarity and content of this project. Your effort to serve me in this way in the midst of your busy schedules was both humbling and inspiring.

All the good folks at Zondervan. I am grateful for your partnership and efforts to republish this book and commit to this series.

Dr. Mohler, for your kind and encouraging words contained in the foreword and your constant prodding of the local church to assume the training of pastors and missionaries.

The faithful saints of Auburndale Baptist Church, who allow me the gift of your fellowship, the encouragement of your love, and your endless support of my labor in the word for the sake of your souls. You model the selflessness required to give up those among us who have been called.

My older brother, Scott, who many years ago loved me enough to challenge my calling when unaccompanied by the affirmation of others. Since then you have remained a wise counselor, inspiring example, and beloved friend to me.

My children—Samuel, Abby, Isabelle, and Claire. What unspeakable joy you bring me by your love, care, and affection. You remain a daily example to me of God's undeserved goodness and grace.

My wife, who remained steadfast in love, encouragement, and support through the approaching deadlines and late nights of writing. Apart from my Savior, there is no one I love more or find more joy in than you.

Our Chief Shepherd, who empowers his shepherds to faithfully shepherd his people until his glorious appearing (1 Peter 5:1–4).

PASTORAL INTERNSHIP TEMPLATE*
Name of Church

Pastoral Internship

(in cooperation with the SBTS applied ministry syllabus and handbook)

Purpose and Benefit

The purpose of this internship is to provide an atmosphere within a local church to train, equip, and affirm men for pastoral ministry. There are five potential benefits in considering this internship:

1. The supportive and loving environment of a local church that assumes responsibility for the care, training, and education of the intern
2. Practical understanding and training for the essential areas of pastoral ministry within the local church
3. An official church position approved by the church that can go on a résumé and reflect ministry experience

---

* This template was designed with Donald Whitney to work in conjunction with the applied ministry courses of The Southern Baptist Theological Seminary. It shows one possible scenario for partnering a pastoral internship with a theological institution. It is, however, not necessary to do so.

4. An opportunity for a local congregation to affirm an individual's gifts and calling
5. Exposure to a pastor's daily schedule to help an individual evaluate and learn more about the pastoral nature of their calling

Duration
Four Months

Compensation
There is no salary for this position.

Hourly Requirements
The position allows for approximately ten hours per week
(Wed: 3:00 p.m. – 7:00 p.m.; Sun: 9:00 a.m. – 12:00 p.m., 5:00 p.m. – 8:00 p.m.)
(Flexible to the intern's needs and availability)

LEARNING OBJECTIVES

General Objectives

- sermon and worship service planning and preparation
- disciplined prayer life
- pastoral care—hospitals, visitation, member care, and membership interviews
- public worship service involvement and evaluation
- funeral services and wedding ceremonies
- leadership meetings (pastors, staff, deacons, committees, etc.)
- essentials of administration
- monthly report to the congregation on personal progress
- two books (in addition to SBTS applied ministry requirements) to read and discuss with pastor or field supervisor (paid for by the church)
- two (five-page) papers (in addition to SBTS applied ministry requirements) to write—theological implications of practical ministry issues

Field Supervisor for SBTS Requirement

Senior pastor

Secondary Supervisor

Other pastors or staff

INTERNSHIP WEEKLY SCHEDULE (FLEXIBLE)

Wednesday

3:00 p.m. – 4:00 p.m.

Meet with pastor: discuss book/paper; time of instruction with learning objectives/personal goals

4:00 p.m. – 5:00 p.m.

Worship service planning with the pastors

5:00 p.m. – 7:00 p.m.

Staff meeting/administration and bookkeeping/Bible study

7:00 p.m. – 8:00 p.m.

Bible study

Sunday

9:00 a.m. – 9:30 a.m.

Meet at church/pray/prepare for Sunday school

9:30 a.m. – 10:30 a.m.

Attend Sunday school

10:45 a.m. – 12:00 p.m.

Morning worship gathering

2:00 p.m. – 5:00 p.m.

Pastors' meetings (monthly)

5:00 p.m. – 5:30 p.m.

Monthly meetings — deacons/committees/membership interviews/etc.

Pastoral Internship Template

5:30 p.m. – 6:00 p.m.

Prepare for evening gathering

6:00 p.m. – 7:00 p.m.

Evening worship gathering

7:15 p.m. – 8:00 p.m.

Worship service review

SERVICE REVIEW EVALUATION[*]

Setting

Service review takes place as a roundtable discussion with one primary facilitator to evaluate the public gatherings for that Lord's Day. It works best to meet fifteen minutes after our evening service, with a duration of forty-five minutes to an hour. There are two main benefits to meeting right after the service: (1) everyone is already at church before going home for the day, and (2) the gatherings for that Lord's Day are fresh on everyone's minds and hearts, which produces a more engaged evaluation. During this time, wives and children have the option of staying and fellowshipping with each other while the men meet. Out of sensitivity to families that are waiting, this meeting should not exceed one hour in length. Anyone is invited to attend, but this is primarily attended by those men who participate in leading and preaching in the public gathering, or who aspire to do so. Those leading and preaching that day, as well as current pastoral interns, are required to attend.

---

[*] I was first exposed to this idea through my friend and mentor, Mark Dever, and the ministry of Capitol Hill Baptist Church in Washington, DC. I have tweaked it over the years, but very little originated with me.

Service Review Evaluation

Purpose

The primary role of service review is twofold:

1. Service review is a safeguard to maintain biblical fidelity within the public gatherings of the church.
2. Service review is a tool to cultivate the skill of giving and receiving sincere, helpful, and godly criticism, which does not come naturally. It must be learned, taught, and molded into believers.

Within these two chief purposes, there are several other purposes to be accomplished in setting this time aside to evaluate:

- to provide an opportunity to speak words of encouragement, as well as correction if needed, into the lives of those who led and preached in the public gathering
- to create a culture of evaluating the public gatherings, not by preference or style, but biblically, theologically, pastorally, and practically
- to create an environment for evaluating with careful judgment what is important and what is not important with regard to sermons and services
- to create an environment for those participating and observing in which they can learn, grow, and mature in the various roles discussed
- to learn discernment in what are helpful, instructive comments—and what are not
- to create an environment of humility, trust, fellowship, and openness with those present

Process

The facilitator's role is much like a moderator or chairman. He is to keep the discussion progressing in a helpful direction and protect the group from digressing in a negative manner. The facilitator asks a question about the service or sermon and goes around the table soliciting thoughts and comments about that particular question. Here are a few examples:

- Did the service run on one continuous theme that led into the preaching of the word?
- What encouraging comments do you have for those who led the service?
- What could have been done better?
- Do you have any theological concerns with the songs chosen?
- Did the congregation seem to sing well? Why or why not?
- What was one truth prayed in the service that was particularly meaningful to you?
- Was the Lord's Table administered in a biblically appropriate way?
- Were there any distractions that need to be mentioned?
- What connections did you see to the Scripture readings and the sermon?
- What is something you learned in the exposition of the text that you didn't notice before?
- What application from the sermon was particularly meaningful to you?
- Was there any portion of the sermon that you would suggest amending or condensing?

- Were there any errors spoken, or clarifications that need to be made, by those who led or preached?

The facilitator can also use this time to have a short discussion about a topic if he feels it would benefit the group. Topics could include approaches to preaching a certain text, factors in determining songs, methods of applying texts edifyingly and faithfully, good templates to think through when praying publicly, and techniques for communicating effectively (e.g., voice inflection). All of these are useful conversations to have with those leading, preaching, and aspiring to do so in your congregation.

This approach should leave attendees challenged to think through different issues that have to do with the public gatherings of your church, but ultimately this time should encourage those who labored in leading and preaching, unless a particularly poor job was done. If you find these meetings have a more faultfinding feel than a spirit of mutual edification, you should consider whether this time has taken a negative direction and then make the appropriate adjustments.

"THE EXTERNAL CALL"

Acts 13:1–3

A Sermon Preached at Auburndale Baptist Church,
Louisville, Kentucky, December 14, 2008[*]

Introduction

There is arguably no equal to Charles Bridges's assessment of
the call of God on someone's life and the responsibility of those
involved. In his book *The Christian Ministry*, Bridges clearly
places the responsibility of one's call into the ministry on the
conscience of the individual and the local church to which
they are committed. Bridges calls this evaluation process the
internal and external call of God as he writes:

> *The external call* is a commission received from and rec-
> ognized by the Church ... not indeed qualifying the
> Minister, but accrediting him, whom God had internally
> and suitably qualified. This call communicates therefore
> only official authority. *The internal call* is the voice and
> power of the Holy Ghost, directing the will and the judg-
> ment, and conveying personal qualifications. Both calls,
> however — though essentially distinct in their character
> and source — are indispensable for the exercise of our
> commission.[27]

---

[*] This sermon was preached at a commissioning service for two
families — one being sent to the mission field and the other to be the
senior pastor of a local church.

Bridges is saying that for an individual to know he is called by God to serve in the ministry, there must be an internal call, which is the desire within an individual to do the work of the ministry and their own conviction that they have been gifted and empowered by God's Spirit to do so.

However, there must also be an external call, which is simply the affirmation from a local church that this person possesses the gifts and godly character suitable for a Christian minister. Charles Bridges, Charles Spurgeon, and many other godly men whom God used in the past to raise up those called into the ministry all agree that both internal and external calls are important for a person to possess to enter into the work of the ministry.

Unfortunately, this process is mostly lost today. And so we as a church this morning should not only consider this great responsibility because of the counsel of Bridges but also because this seems to be how the early church and those throughout church history operated as they recognized, affirmed, and sent those whom God was clearly calling.

Last week, we referenced the special relationship between those who go and those who stay. Luther Rice described this as "rope holding." When someone is lowered into a well or cave, someone must hold the rope, or else the person cannot be lowered. If the rope holder at any time drops the rope, the person in the well cannot be brought back up. This is a picture of what it means for the local church to send missionaries to the field and support them continually until their work is done and they safely return home.

Luther Rice held the rope for Adoniram Judson; Andrew

Fuller held the rope for William Carey; and these two families sit here this morning because they are grabbing the rope that we as a church are extending for them to take from us as we send one to the mission field and the other into the pastorate. We will consider what that looks like for us as a church in a few moments, but before we do that, let us consider arguably the best example of this in Scripture—the time when the church in Antioch affirms and sends Saul and Barnabas out to do the work they had been set apart by God to do. Therefore, our core passage we are going to work from this morning is this example we find in the beginning of Acts 13.

Let me set the context of where we step into the book of Acts. Jesus has come, lived a perfect life, died on the cross, rose from the dead three days later, and in this accomplished work satisfied God's wrath and purchased salvation from sin with his own blood. Therefore, whoever would call on Christ in faith, repent, and give their lives to him would receive salvation. The book of Acts is the result of this gospel—this good news—of Jesus saving sinners being preached by his followers and his church being built.

Chapter 13 marks a turning point in Acts. The first twelve chapters focus mostly on Peter, and the remaining chapters focus on Paul. In the first twelve chapters the focus was on the Jerusalem and Judean church being established. The rest of Acts is focused on the spread of the Gentile church throughout the world. Luke shows us how this sovereign purpose of God in building his church continues as Saul and Barnabas return from Jerusalem to be officially commissioned for God's purposes by the church in Antioch.

"The External Call"

> Now in the church at Antioch there were prophets and teachers: Barnabas, Simeon called Niger, Lucius of Cyrene, Manaen (who had been brought up with Herod the tetrarch) and Saul. While they were worshiping the Lord and fasting, the Holy Spirit said, "Set apart for me Barnabas and Saul for the work to which I have called them." So after they had fasted and prayed, they placed their hands on them and sent them off.
>
> Acts 13:1–3

Let us first consider the biblical warrant for the external call and then determine our responsibility to it as a congregation.

The External Call of God (Acts 13:1–3)

The external call of God can only be given by the church, and any effort to place this great responsibility on anyone or anything else risks the health and well-being of local churches and ultimately the witness of Christ. The external call has practically vanished in the twentieth and now the twenty-first century, as many of the students I know on the campus of The Southern Baptist Theological Seminary have admitted to me that their home church wasn't involved (or as involved) in their decision to pursue ministry.

It is time for the local church to once again embrace this enormous responsibility to test, train, affirm, and send young pastors and missionaries into the ministry by deliberately examining their gifts and character. This is the local church's call today, and it has been the responsibility of the church from the beginning—as we clearly see the church in Antioch embrace this responsibility and be faithful to it. The church in

Antioch provides a great lesson for how we can better understand the external call in its relation to the local church in our day.

Centered on the Local Church (verse 1)

We see in verse 1 the sole presence of the church at Antioch. There were no seminaries or mission organizations. This is not to say that seminaries and mission organizations aren't ordained by God and aren't helpful. However, what I want us to observe this morning is the fact that in the early church, the testing, training, affirming, and sending of pastors and missionaries was the sole responsibility of the local church and the pastors, leaders, and believers found within it. We see in verse 1 the church at Antioch, and we see their leaders. The prophets and teachers mentioned in verse 1 were the early church pastors and leaders. This is the central platform on which God reveals his will for Saul and Barnabas—through the other pastors and believers of the church in Antioch.

Recognized by the Pastors (verses 2–3)

Verse 2 shows us these leaders doing what they normally did— they were worshiping the Lord and fasting. In other words, they were doing the work of the church in preaching and teaching God's word and shepherding the church and being deliberately prayerful about it. Let's remember what fasting is. Fasting is the purposeful setting aside of eating to concentrate on spiritual issues, predominately through prayer. It is in the faithfulness of these leaders that the Holy Spirit reveals in verse 2 God's will for Saul and Barnabas. They are to be set apart for God for the work to which he has called them.

"The External Call"

Let's consider the guidance of God for this decision. First and foremost, they certainly had the message of the Holy Spirit from verse 2, which was unique to the establishment of the early church. But let's also not forget that they also had the fruitfulness of Saul's and Barnabas's previous labor. At the end of Acts 11, Saul and Barnabas had come to the church at Antioch and fellowshipped for an entire year (11:26), met with the church, and cared for them. The church and its leaders had the evidence of God's call on their life also because of the fruitfulness of their past labor among them.

Therefore, we see they are able to affirm them not only by God's guidance by his Spirit but also by their past fruitful labor, all in the wisdom of God through their continual fasting and praying. We see the leaders lay hands on them to affirm them in this call (13:3), which is not just the affirmation of the leaders but an extension of the entire church, which we see in Acts 6 and later in Acts 14.

When colleges send people to recruit for their basketball team, they are not sending their baseball or football coaches. They are not even sending one of their basketball players. They are sending one of the coaches who has, first of all, demonstrated his ability to play basketball in the past and has also shown his level of evaluating other talent by his maturity in his knowledge of the game. In the same way, it is a pastor who initially recognizes the potential calling of a young pastor for them to be tested and trained within the congregation.

Affirmed by the Local Church (verse 3)

As we consider the Antioch church, the church and its leaders have been able to watch the lives of Saul and Barnabas and see their fruitful ministry within this particular church. They sought the Lord's guidance, as they now officially apply the external call of God on Saul and Barnabas and place their hands on them in affirmation on behalf of the church (verse 3). And then, as the end of verse 3 tells us, they "sent them off." Also notice how the Spirit is working through the church— the church sends them off in verse 3, but verse 4 tells us that they were "sent on their way by the Holy Spirit." Not only is the church's involvement implied, but when Saul and Barnabas return to report in Acts 14, they "gathered the church together and reported all that God had done through them" (Acts 14:27).

All of this was to lead the leaders (prophets and teachers) and the church by the Holy Spirit to play some role in giving the external call to Saul and Barnabas for them to do the work to which God had called them. How do we measure the importance of this affirmation from the Antioch church to choose the properly called men for this task? It results in God continuing to build his church through the hearing of the gospel by Gentiles—and thus the church is built throughout the Roman province and the world.

The Responsibility of the Local Church

This event in Acts 13 provides a simple picture for us, but it doesn't give specific examples on how to test and train appropriately so that local church pastors and the congregation can affirm to send. Therefore, in our remaining time, I want to consider four specific ways we can be deliberate about how Auburndale Baptist Church can be equipped to grant an external call in an individual's life, specifically these two families

104

who sit here before us—one to be sent to the mission field, the other into the pastorate.

Testing

We know from Paul that God gives to the church apostles, prophets, evangelists, and pastors and teachers for the equipping and building up of the church (Ephesians 4:11–12). Therefore, the best way to find them is to test those who feel an internal calling to this work. The best way to test men for the office of pastor is through the qualifications for this office clearly mapped out in Scripture (1 Timothy 3:1–7; Titus 1:5–9). Through these characteristics listed, we can begin to determine whether a young man desiring this work is called, especially through testing his gift to preach and teach. This is a testing that is done visibly before the congregation.

For example, we had twelve different men preach on a psalm on Sunday evenings this past summer, which provided an opportunity for them to serve our church and also supplied a way for their preaching gifts to be tested before the entire church. These brothers are also tested when they go and visit you in your home. Not only are they caring for you and the church in coming to see you, but they are also being tested in a pastoral moment—how self-controlled, hospitable, gentle, peaceful, above reproach, and respectable they are, all of which are qualities that Paul highlights (1 Timothy 3:1–7; Titus 1:5–9).

Training

Training is testing that becomes a little more deliberate. In this stage, the pastors of the church have identified to some degree the gifts in someone reflected from 1 Timothy 3:1–7, and these gifts need to be deliberately tested and trained through practical experience. This is where a brother begins to play a more active role in the leadership of the church by regularly teaching a class or preaching for a whole month on Sunday evenings. This person becomes someone the pastors begin to trust to send to a hospital on his own and to get more exposure to the decisions and directions of the church. This is someone who is involved in evaluating the sermons and the services every week. In all these efforts, these brothers are being trained for ministry while the members of the church continue to be served, encouraged, and cared for through their efforts.

_____ [missionary family], you have been in many of our homes and us in yours. We have had the joy of fellowship with you. You have served our church in so many ways. _____ [both wives], you have cared for our children as you have faithfully cared for your own. You modeled a Christlike attitude through a very difficult family schedule. _____ [husbands of both families], you have preached and taught God's word to us. You have helped several people grow spiritually through your counseling efforts. You have helped lead our public gatherings and have used your pastoral experience to help the pastors think through some difficult issues.

However, as we fellowshipped together and served with you both, something else was happening—you were being tested and trained before our eyes for the work to which you felt called. In God's kind providence, he has allowed our church the joy of Christian fellowship with you through that time to put us in a place to be able to affirm you.

"The External Call"

Affirming

Once the pastors and leaders have had adequate time to test and train a brother pursuing this office, the time comes to either affirm them or not affirm them. If the pastors feel a brother has been qualified for this office, we then recommend them to the congregation to also evaluate this individual. Because much of this testing and training is visibly done before the people and with the people, the congregation has now been, hopefully, informed enough to make their own decision. This has resulted in very helpful and fruitful discussions in our members' meetings, and if there are no concerns about the pastors' recommendation, the church comes back after another month of praying to vote.

This affirmation can come in different ways—it may be affirmation for a brother to serve as an assistant pastor here in our church; it may be for someone who is leaving to pursue a ministry position or for a couple to go to the mission field. Regardless of the scenario, the decision to ordain a brother as a pastor or missionary is the final step before we send someone with the full support and external call of Auburndale Baptist Church.

_____ [missionary family], I have had one-on-one meetings with you to discuss your marriage, family, school challenges, and struggles with sin. The pastors have discussed your situation on numerous occasions. We have had several public discussions about you at members' meetings. Yet, you still sit here because in all those discussions, we as a church have felt convinced, though the road you face will be hard, that this is the work to which the Lord has called you.

_____ [pastor family], as a pastor of this congregation you have already been tested, trained, and affirmed. However, you sit here because this congregation is deeply confident that you are equipped to face the unique challenges of the church you have been asked to pastor because of the faithfulness you've shown as you met challenges in our church as a pastor of this congregation. In a few moments, we will do what the church in Antioch did (Acts 13:3) — we will lay hands on each of you and pray as a way of sealing our affirmation of you to pursue these opportunities by God's grace.

Sending

It can be a complicated and involved process to send someone out. Whether it is someone pursuing a pastorate or service in missions, we as a church in sending them are committing to regularly pray for them, possibly give wisdom and pastoral oversight in where they should go, and then be in regular contact with them while in the field. The church may need to make a commitment to financially support them, especially in the case of a missionary going into the field who must raise his own financial support. Sending is not the end of the process but the beginning of a new commitment we as a local church give those who have been called, tested, trained, affirmed, and sent out from among us.

Application for Our Church

As we consider our responsibility as a church, we must realize that each of us has a responsibility if our church is to be faithful to the external call. If you are one who desires the work of a pastor or missionary, Paul says this is a noble task (1 Timothy 3:1).

"The External Call"

Yet, your responsibility is not simply to rely on your internal call, but to place yourself under the authority of the local church and trust that God will work through the pastors and believers in this congregation to affirm your internal call with an external call.

If you are not someone feeling this call, then your responsibility is to do what so many of you do well as faithful church members — to invest and pour your life into each other so that when the time comes to affirm, you are well-informed. Come on Sunday evenings to hear these different brothers preach. Approach them afterward and encourage them with insights into what you thought they did well, and lovingly correct them in areas where they can improve. Put your personal preferences aside on which of them you like better as a preacher and embrace the opportunity someone else gets. If we each play the part God has for us, we will be encouraged and our church will be built. We will guard the gospel more faithfully, and we will have a great faith in whatever God's will is for each opportunity we have as a local church to grant an external call.

In our world today, someone does not have to have an external call to go into the ministry. But in a church that embraces the external call, in a church that sees the necessity, in a church that realizes what is at stake — a church like Antioch — I submit to you that God is honored and a biblically faithful church will be found in those who desire to conduct themselves according to God's design and purposes.

NOTES

1. Quoted in Adrian Warnock's blog post, "Interview with Dr. Albert Mohler," November 8, 2006, http://adrianwarnock.com/2006/11/interview-dr-albert-mohler-radio-host.htm (accessed October 15, 2013).
2. Charles Bridges, *The Christian Ministry: An Inquiry into the Causes of Its Inefficiency* (Edinburgh: Banner of Truth, 1967), 91–92.
3. Quoted in *Leadership* journal, "Leader's Insight: Get-It-Done Leadership: Interview with Andy Stanley," May 2007, www.christianitytoday.com/le/currenttrendscolumns/leadershipweekly/cln70528.html?start=2 (accessed October 15, 2013).
4. The biblical office of pastor is synonymous with the terms *elder, overseer,* and *bishop* throughout the New Testament and refers to the appointed shepherd of the New Testament church.
5. Jim Cromarty, *King of the Cannibals: The Story of John G. Paton, Missionary to the New Hebrides* (Darlington, UK: Evangelical Press, 1997), 65.
6. James Montgomery Boice, *Acts: An Expositional Commentary* (Grand Rapids: Baker, 1997), 226.
7. Titus 1:6–9 and 1 Peter 5:1–4 are also clear complementary passages describing these biblical qualifications, though 1 Timothy 3:1–7 is the primary passage of focus for this chapter.
8. Richard Baxter, *The Reformed Pastor* (Edinburgh: Banner of Truth, 2001), 53.
9. C. H. Spurgeon, *Lectures to My Students* (Grand Rapids: Zondervan, 1954), 26.
10. Ibid., 26–27.
11. Michael A. G. Haykin, Roger D. Duke, and A. James Fuller, *Soldiers of Christ: Selections from the Writings of Basil Manly, Sr. and Basil Manly, Jr.* (Cape Coral, FL: Founders Press, 2009), 175–76.
12. Spurgeon, *Lectures to My Students*, 26.
13. Thomas K. Ascol, ed., *Dear Timothy: Letters on Pastoral Ministry* (Cape Coral, FL: Founders Press, 2004), 272.
14. Haykin, Duke, and Fuller, *Soldiers of Christ*, 174.
15. David Dickson, *The Elder and His Work* (Phillipsburg, NJ: P & R, 2004), 30–31.
16. John L. Dagg, *Manual of Theology: A Treatise on Church Order* (Charleston, SC: Southern Baptist Publication Society, 1859), 248.

Notes

17. Traditional Protestantism defined a true church by true preaching of the word, proper observance of the sacraments, and faithful exercise of church discipline (see Edmund P. Clowney, *The Church* [Downers Grove, IL: InterVarsity, 1995], 101).

18. Quoted in James M. Garretson, *Princeton and Preaching: Archibald Alexander and the Christian Ministry* (Carlisle, PA: Banner of Truth, 2005), 55.

19. Mark Dever, *Nine Marks of a Healthy Church* (Wheaton, IL: Crossway, 2000), 26.

20. Dagg, *Manual of Theology*, 274.

21. For a helpful example, see Mark Dever and Paul Alexander, *The Deliberate Church: Building Your Ministry on the Gospel* (Wheaton, IL: Crossway, 2005), 158–59.

22. Haykin, Duke, and Fuller, *Soldiers of Christ*, 174.

23. Arnold Dallimore, *George Whitefield: The Life and Times of the Great Evangelist of the 18th Century Revival* (Carlisle, PA: Banner of Truth, 2001), 1:549.

24. Ibid., 1:550.

25. Ibid.

26. John Flavel, "The Character of a Complete Evangelical Pastor, Drawn by Christ," in *The Works of John Flavel* (Carlisle, PA: Banner of Truth, 1997), 6:579.

27. Bridges, *Christian Ministry*, 91–92.

Practical
Shepherding

The Practical Shepherding series provides pastors and ministry leaders with practical help to do the work of pastoral ministry in a local church. The seven-volume series, when complete, will include:

- *Conduct Gospel-Centered Funerals: Applying the Gospel at the Unique Challenges of Death*

- *Prepare Them to Shepherd: Test, Train, Affirm, and Send the Next Generation of Leaders*

- *Visit the Sick: Ministering God's Grace in Times of Illness*

- *Comfort the Grieving: Ministering God's Grace in Times of Loss* (Available February 2015)

- *Understand, Plan, and Lead Worship: Applying Biblical Doctrine and Spirituality to Christian Worship* (Available February 2015)

- *Pray for the Flock: Ministering God's Grace through Intercession* (Available August 2015)

- *Exercise Oversight: Shepherding the Flock through Administration and Delegation* (Available August 2015)

In addition to the series, be sure to look for these titles by Brian and Cara Croft on the pastor's family and ministry:

- *The Pastor's Family* by Brian and Cara Croft

- *The Pastor's Ministry* by Brian Croft (Available April 2015)